CONSUMING PASSIONS

Help for Compulsive Shoppers

ELLEN MOHR CATALANO
& NINA SONENBERG

NEW HARBINGER PUBLICATIONS, INC.

Copyright © 1993 by New Harbinger Publications, Inc.
5674 Shattuck Avenue
Oakland, CA 94609

Library of Congress Catalog Card Number: 93-083369
ISBN 1-879237-38-5 paperback
ISBN 1-879237-39-3 hardcover

The chart on page 211 is reprinted with the permission of IDS Financial Services Inc.

All rights reserved.
Printed in the United States of America on recycled paper.
Edited by Kirk Johnson
Cover Design by SHELBY DESIGNS & ILLUSTRATES

1st Printing 1993 8,000 copies

I dedicate this book in memory of my mother, Wanda Regier Mohr, 1926-1992.

—E.M.C.

With love to my mother, and to the memory of my father.

—N.S.

Contents

Acknowledgments

I gratefully wish to acknowledge Dr. John Schroll for his assistance and emotional support; Dr. Sarah Drennan for her ideas and enthusiasm; and the many people who, with courage and generosity, shared their shopping experiences as we prepared this book.

—E.M.C.

Special thanks to Dr. Matthew McKay for method and insight, and to Pat Fanning, Kirk Johnson, and the crew at New Harbinger for all the editorial wisdom and stress relief.

—N.S.

Introduction

Remember the old days at the drive-in when they flashed pictures of popcorn on the screen? What were you compelled to do? Rush to the concession stand to buy some! It wasn't long before the association between movie going and popcorn eating grew to become an almost unbreakable combination.

This book is about examining your own conscious and unconscious associations with spending—and about breaking the spending habits that you feel are harmful to you. Did you open this book out of a sense of guilt, because you know you should understand your buying habits better? Or do you know someone close to you, a friend or a loved one, who sometimes spends uncontrollably and whom you think this book might help?

"Addiction" and "compulsion" have become popular words lately. Too popular, say some critics, charging that almost all modern Americans see themselves as addicted to *something*. But the trend to self-examination and the desire for self-improvement— no matter what names we choose to give them—can be seen as signs that we are willing to reassess our priorities and set new and reasonable limits for ourselves. Many books are on the shelves, and a variety of groups meet in each community, to address addictive behaviors and teach recovery. These resources are clearly filling a need, although the wealth of models to choose from and psychological gurus to follow can seem bewildering.

This book aims to present you with a reasonable range of choices, rather than one rigid model of addiction or recovery. The material has been developed to help you spot your own problem shopping behaviors and choose a management strategy that you feel you can stick to. If you find it helpful to use the words "addiction" or "compulsion" to describe your hours at the mall, feel free to do so—especially if the terms help you feel that you are on the road to "recovery." If you prefer to think of "problem shopping" (and problem solving), that's fine too.

The focus throughout this book will be on addressing problems in *behavior*, as opposed to dissecting personality traits. Compulsive shopping is something you do, not an inherent part of who you are. At the same time, the problem of compulsive shopping should not be presented in a simplistic manner. Many other forms of compulsive behavior interweave strands of culture, gender, and personality, and compulsive shopping shares this complexity. It is more than a disease or a simple lack of self-control. For this reason, exercises in this book will ask you to reflect on your own history, the culture that surrounds you, and the fears and desires you carry with you from one area of your life to another. Underlying motivations to shop, such as low self-esteem, a sense of inner-emptiness, and a need for danger, can exert much greater power over you when they remain hidden from sight. Bringing these motivations to light is one way to gain a sense of control. Recognizing the underlying reasons that you have for shopping will help you learn to address those reasons *without* resorting to shopping.

Your primary goal in reading this book can be simply described: to feel in control of each and every spending decision you make. Perhaps you will discover that you can look and not buy; perhaps you will discover that you don't even have to go out and look to find the solace you seek. Success in this book will be defined by *you*: you will set your own limits, as you learn from your own shopping history and observe your current shopping patterns.

This book can be a guide, but the answers and the control you seek lie within you. Your progress will be measured by each step you take toward uncovering knowledge about yourself and reclaiming power over your actions.

Are You a Compulsive Shopper?

Compulsive shoppers know who they are. They feel that they must buy things. They are driven to purchase. Some of the things they buy seem necessary, and others seem frivolous. But it doesn't matter if the items actually are necessary or frivolous, because the act of buying is all that counts. It is this act that you will examine here in all of its complexity.

Compulsive shoppers tend to feel driven to spend their money. They don't care where in particular they spend it or what they buy with it. They feel that they "must" go through the act of choosing and spending and will often talk themselves into wanting something, anything. Compulsive shoppers can be great rationalizers, deciding that this or that reason makes it "okay" or "important" that they buy. In reality, they just want to feel the *rush* of purchase. This rush costs them dearly in money, damaged credit ratings, guilt, shame, and secrecy. Most painful can be the feeling that they are "out of control."

At first it will be scary to look closely at your own behavior and begin to uncover your hidden motives. Like any other effort to change, it will require honesty and bravery to face the issues. Perhaps you use shopping to avoid a problem at home. It's far easier to rush to the store than it is to face up to the possibility of a deteriorating marriage or the void of loneliness. Indeed, the process of breaking an addiction may uncover considerable pain that lies beneath the habit. If you find wells of deep emotion as you plumb the depths of your shopping behavior, you may want to consider seeking professional counseling. But at this moment you are faced with a choice. In opening this book and reading this far, you have already entertained the notion that it is time for things to be different. If you don't change a thing, you will simply buy more of the things that you've already bought—and pay the same emotional price for them, right? Is that the choice you are prepared to live with?

Taking Control

If you faithfully follow this step-by-step guide, you will be able to master your problem. No longer will you be a victim of marketing ploys and sales gimmicks. You may be influenced by advertising, but you will feel a sense of control over what you see, hear, and choose to buy, regardless of what the commercials tell you. You will be able to sense when your emotions come into play and when you begin to slip into old behavior in order to avoid dealing with your own issues. And finally, you will NOT be able to blame your spending habits on other people or other problems, such as a crummy job or a lousy family environment.

This book is timely. In the nineties Americans have grown increasingly aware of and perhaps embarrassed by their country's inability to manage its own budget. Perhaps some take a small consolation from seeing their personal spending habits reflected in the country's problem at large. But this nation is made up of individuals' problems. And you are not alone. Millions of American men and women experience daily the frustrations of overspending. Consumer credit counselors report burgeoning requests for help. Government statistics document an ongoing and significant increase in consumer debt from one year to the next.

The nineties have moved us as a nation into the global realization that we cannot continue to spend recklessly, neither as a nation nor as individuals.

The past decade has also seen more and more women continue to enter the work force, both out of choice and just to meet the basic survival needs of food and housing. As women acquire their own sources of income, they become increasingly aware of the forces that seek to part them from their money. Men, meanwhile, are contending with salaries that cannot maintain the lifestyles that their fathers managed a generation ago, when one paycheck was enough to support a family. This book comes at a time when men and women alike realize the need for greater control of their financial resources in order to meet personal and professional goals.

Out of the Closet: Some Famous Shoppers

Let it be said that compulsive shopping is not unique to this century, although the problem has mushroomed in an economy built on infinite consumer desire. But if today we discover Imelda Marcos with a closet of 1,060 pairs of shoes, the last century discovered Mary Todd Lincoln, who felt that she had to order 84 pairs of gloves before she could move into the White House in comfort. Once she got there, Mary Todd redecorated the White House with the same tireless gusto as Jackie Kennedy, a famous first-lady shopper of our day. And just as Imelda Marcos was humiliated by a mocking press corps ("If conspicuous consumption were a federal offense, Imelda Marcos would be a shoe-in for two life-terms," remarked *U.S. News and World Report* in 1990, commenting on Imelda's acquittal on charges of theft from the Philippine treasury), Mary Todd was the talk of the Union for her extravagant expenses ("A Mania for Shopping!" screamed a *Chicago Times* headline in the 1870s). Indeed, Mary Todd met with less legal fortune than Imelda. She was humiliated in a public insanity trial and ultimately declared insane as a result of charges brought by her son based on her spending behavior.

Believe it or not, the century before that gives us yet another great shopper: George Washington! "Another of George's hidden talents was buying things," writes historian Marvin Kitman in his book *The Making of the President, 1789*. "His favorite indoor sport was shopping for clothes.... He loved to design fancy uniforms and the accoutrements." Washington also spent lavishly on himself and his wife, buying the finest materials he could find in great quantity from the day of their marriage. "He had a consuming passion. The most awesome achievement in the newlywed's incredible shopping spree was his buying by mail in June, 1768, a new chariot." ("In the newest taste, handsome, genteel, and light...")

What's more, Washington bought it all on credit. "He charged everything he ordered from merchants to his account," writes Kitman. "Instead of using MasterCard or Visa, he consigned his tobacco or other cash crops to his creditors, which they would sell as his agents. The difference he had to pay, or send more tobacco to cover." Have you guessed the bad news? "Despite all his accounts, perhaps because of them, he was always in debt... No matter how bad his financial plight at Mount Vernon, even when he was appalled by the size of his debt, he didn't stop spending extravagantly." Then, as now—despite all our own stereotypes—men were as susceptible to compulsive shopping as women. (For more entertaining reading about Washington, see Kitman's *The Making of the President 1789* and *George Washington's Expense Account*. After eight years of war against the British, and after refusing a salary of $48,000, Washington turned in an expense account for $449,261.51!) Perhaps Americans of every century and gender can identify with the words of one infamous 20th-century shopper: "My shopping demons are hopping."

In This Book...

People almost always laugh on first hearing about compulsive shopping, an idea that will be explored in chapter 1, "The Smiled-Upon Addiction." But, as history reveals—and your own knowledge confirms—it is a grave problem for many people, with frightening personal and social consequences. At the very least, you'll already have learned from this book that you're in good company. Chapter 2, "Are You a Compulsive Shopper?" will help you determine just where in the wide range of shopping behaviors your own problem resides.

Compulsive shopping is a problem that connects you to your society: you can't shop alone in your closet. While you gain nothing by blaming society or any other outside force for your problems, you can benefit tremendously from a clear-eyed view of the many pressures in this society to shop. Examining our "shop till you drop" culture from a detached perspective will help make it easier for you to make your own decisions about spending and stick with them no matter what the ads tell you. This is the aim of chapter 3, "How Our Culture Helps You Shop."

The real work of self-examination and change begins with chapter 4, "Discovering Why You Shop." Both this chapter and the two that follow, "Keeping Track of Shopping Behaviors" and "Learning From Your Shopping Record," will guide you through a step-by-step process of self-discovery. The more earnestly and openly you approach the exercises and ideas presented here, the more resources you will have to negotiate your change.

No strategy for change is complete without offering support techniques and positive alternatives to your habit. A few simple techniques, such as those offered in chapter 7, "Anxiety and Stress Relief," can make a tremendous difference in your approach to shopping (and other life tasks). No longer will you have to look to shopping to relieve stress; indeed, these free, go-anywhere techniques can take the edge off the anxiety you already feel and keep new anxiety (and anxiety-producing bills!) from mounting. And relaxation breaks are just one alternative to shopping. If you have a hard time imagining *anything* else you'd enjoy, look again. Chapter 8, "Alternatives to Shopping: From A to Z," offers alternatives for every letter of the alphabet. This book may not just be the end of an old habit, but the beginning of something new and wonderful.

Change that lasts involves redefining both your behavior and your outlook. To help you begin to see the world around you in a new light, chapter 9, "Fighting Back," includes some novel ideas on how to watch TV, how to read a catalog, and—most importantly—how to survive a mall. These exercises were designed to be as entertaining as they are instructive.

Chapter 10, "Taking Control of Your Finances," is a crucial step in the recovery-planning stage. Written by financial planner Glenn Catalano, it offers no-nonsense advice about how to recover from your current situation and move forward with self-discipline and confidence. Rather than seeing a budget as a constraint, you will learn to see it as a ticket to freedom—from panic, from angry creditors, from your money problems. The shopping maintenance plan in chapter 11, "When the Going Gets Tough," will seal these changes, drawing on ideas throughout this book and setting you up for lasting success.

Think of this book as your stepping stone. It does not have all the answers: you find them yourself as you move forward. The ideas and exercises in the book will support you in your progress and help you reach your own will, wisdom, and desire for change. With these forces, there is no problem you cannot resolve.

1

The Smiled-Upon Addiction

Did this chapter title make you shudder or cringe at the thought of having an "addiction"? Doesn't the word conjure up dimly lit hallways, hypodermic needles, and desperate-looking people without resources or hope? In fact, over half of America's substance abusers come from middle class homes of educated people with jobs. The word "addict" no longer has the implications it once did. Today knowledge about addictive behavior has spread so widely that there are many more sympathetic ears than critical ones. Indeed, it's been said that America is becoming addicted to the idea of addiction.

Of course, it's one thing to understand all this, and another to think that the term addiction might apply to *you*. For this reason you may be tempted to walk away from the subject, to throw this book down and read no further. Walking away is a natural reaction—especially when a behavior that seems natural and necessary to you is questioned and criticized. Even if you suspect that your behavior may be excessive, the idea of labelling it "addictive" or "compulsive" may feel so uncomfortable or demeaning or threatening that it seems easier just to ignore your suspicions and pretend that the behavior doesn't exist. But stick it out, at least to the end of this chapter. Once at the end, ask yourself: "Do I still want to walk away?" Chances are you will feel less tense about the meaning of addiction and more willing to read on.

Even though addiction is still a dirty word to some people, it has certainly come out of the closet in the last decade. It sometimes seems that America is on a quest to eradicate addictions. One addiction resource book lists 94 national organizations which can be contacted for help and information, ranging from Sex Addicts Anonymous to Gamblers Anonymous. With all these groups springing up everywhere, the nature and meaning of addiction can seem confusing. You may ask, what exactly is an "addiction," and what does it have to do with problem shopping behavior?

The Evolution of the Addiction Movement

Consider, first, addiction to alcohol. America's most popular way to manage alcohol addiction is Alcoholics Anonymous (AA), whose program has served as model for managing many other types of addictions. The current AA model originated in 1939, offering total abstinence and group support as a way for alcoholics to stay sober. The organization's membership grew rapidly, doubling in size in the 1980s alone to a worldwide membership of 1.7 million, as recently reported by David Streitfeld in the *Washington Post*. AA's model spawned many offspring, such as AlaTeen, Drugs Anonymous, Food Addicts Anonymous, and Obsessive-Compulsives Anonymous.

Based on a set of guidelines called the "Twelve Steps," AA and its offshoots work from an established process that has had tremendous impact on how this society views addiction. The Steps begin as one admits powerlessness over the group's addiction problem and acknowledges that life has become unmanageable as a result of it. Further on, one admits that a power greater than oneself can restore sanity. Before one can gain control over the progressive nature of addiction, according to this model, one must fully embrace these concepts.

Many of these programs argue that addictions of all kinds are illnesses and that alcoholism in particular is a genetically linked disease. It seems clear that compulsive shopping is *not* a genetically borne disease (unless in the future someone discovers a shopping gene!). Current thinking, however, submits that addictive behaviors of all kinds have more similarities than differences, no matter what the substance or behavior abused. Physical dependency is an exception, but it is one factor among many. Compulsive shopping, like other addictive behaviors, is a complex interweaving of family influences, cultural conditioning, and personal coping skills which are learned early in childhood and carried into adulthood.

Other Insights

In this book you will see the following words used interchangeably to describe out-of-control shopping: compulsive shopping, problem shopping, shopping addiction, habitual shopping. Should you choose to read further about addictions, you will also see other terms to describe addictive behavior:

obsession	impulse control disorder
dependency	co-dependency
excessive	abusive
discomfort anxiety	low-frustration tolerance

What are the differences between these terms, if any? Comparing the terms "compulsion" and "addiction," for example, Dr. Charles Whitfield, author of such popular books on co-dependency as *Healing the Child Within* and *Co-Dependence, Healing the Human Condition*, says that while it may be difficult to differentiate some compulsions from addictions, one important difference is that "compulsions tend to have less severe consequences." He uses the example of a person who is compulsively neat, who is unlikely to endure the severe outcomes experienced by individuals who drink excessively.

Craig Nakken, a family therapist from Minnesota, defines addiction as a "pathological love and trust relationship with an object or event." In this case, *pathological* means "abnormal" or "unhealthy." Addicted individuals put abnormal love and trust into a relationship with things or an experience, rather than seeking to meet their needs by establishing healthy relationships with people. In other words, they put booze or shopping or gambling first, over friends or family.

One model of addiction, based on "rational-emotive" theory, suggests that a particularly low threshold for pain or frustration is present in most addicts. According to this theory, the addict has the irrational belief that he or she cannot survive pain, discomfort, or unpleasantness and must avoid these sensations at all costs. Theorists of this school, such as researchers Raymond DiGiuseppe and John McInerney, have labelled this phenomenon "low-frustration tolerance." They call the acute fear experienced by addicts at the prospect of such pain "discomfort anxiety."

According to this theory, all addicts—whether addicted to cocaine or shopping—experience similar emotions, fears, and anxiety at the prospect of being cut off from their addiction—of not being able to do drugs or shop when they feel the urge. This terror of pain and discomfort is what actually causes them to engage in the habit. Even though they know that their behavior will be destructive in the long run, the feeling is that they have no choice: they must engage in the habit because they cannot survive without the immediate relief it will provide.

A clear and all-encompassing way to look at addiction is offered in Stanton Peele's book, *The Meaning of Addiction*:

> Addiction is best understood as an individual's
> adjustment, albeit a self-defeating one, to his or
> her environment. It represents an habitual style of
> coping, albeit one that the individual is capable of
> modifying with changing psychological and life
> circumstances.

Peele suggests that addictive behavior is a way you've found to cope with life. Even though these coping skills may be unhealthy and unproductive, they are still a way of adjusting to your environment. You've repeated your bad habits so often, that they become second nature. The good news Peele offers is that bad habits can be unlearned and that all of us are capable of changing our emotional and life circumstances.

The distinctions between these definitions are not crucial. The point is to realize that you have a problem that feels out of control, regardless of how you define it.

Underlying Traits and Motivations

Professors Thomas O'Guinn and Ronald Faber, pioneer researchers in the field of compulsive buying, agree that while there is inconsistency in the labelling of compulsive behaviors, all the labels point to common features and related phenomena. Above all, they note, the behaviors are repetitive and problematic for the individual. Other traits they have encountered often in their research pool of compulsive shoppers include:

- Feeling a drive, impulse, or urge to shop

- Feeling dependent on shopping

- Tending to deny the harmful consequences

- Repeatedly trying and failing to control behavior

- Having a low sense of self-worth, especially when considering behavior

- Using shopping to cope with stress, escape demands and pressure, and to overcome unpleasant emotions or situations

Such a list can be helpful in identifying compulsive behavior: perhaps you recognize yourself in some of the characteristics above. But the list stops at describing observable behavior. Another way to consider addictions is to look at the motivations that may have given rise to the behavior in the first place and that serve to keep the addiction going. When considered in this light, a new series of common features that addictions share comes into focus. Whether you are addicted to drugs, alcohol, gambling, shopping, or relationships—or whether you're not sure you're addicted to anything at all—the discussion that follows may help you identify some of your own underlying traits and motivations.

1. Addiction can be a defense against anxiety, fear, pain, and other negative emotions. When emotions seem too much to bear, addiction provides an escape. If you can distract yourself from negative feelings by shopping, you put off having to face your anger, your fear, or your pain. Often these emotions run deep, perhaps triggered by old childhood wounds; the addict would rather substitute absorption in an addiction than reexperience the pain of these old hurts. Perhaps you felt that the only time you got attention from your parents as a child was when they bought you things—and so you equated love with things. When you feel pangs of loneliness or low self-esteem, rather than thinking about the emotional love and support you missed, you simply buy yourself more things. The trigger for an addictive episode can also be simple: you're frustrated from being held up in traffic, so you go to the mall to "escape." But sometimes "simple" triggers mask deeper needs.

Fear of abandonment is a powerful negative emotion common to compulsive shoppers. In this society of plenty, the compulsive shopper often feels that he or she must hoard things, even things that will never be used. This may well reflect a fear of going without and being left alone. Carolyn Wesson, author of *Women Who Shop Too Much*, explains that children who fear abandonment throughout their childhood are unable to develop a strong sense of inner security. They act out their "inner loneliness" by bringing in as many supporting goods from the outside as they can. The acquisition of things becomes a distraction from the pain of loneliness and insecurity.

2. Addiction can be a defense against shame and feelings of low self-worth. Underneath an addiction may lie a sense that you are inadequate. Perhaps you experienced rejection as a teenager or felt profound embarrassment as a child. Young people often translate this painful experience to mean: "I must not be good enough. I deserve to be treated rottenly." Whether this is a conscious or an unconscious experience, you carry its demeaning effects into adulthood. Feeling inadequate on the inside, you search for support and status from the outside. It seems that purchasing just the right dress or piece of jewelry will magically give you self-worth. And the search goes on and on.

Perfectionists often fall into this trap. No matter what successes and accomplishments they achieve, underneath it all they say to themselves, "I don't measure up, so I must look perfect, live in the right neighborhood, and drive a status car in order to tell the world that I'm worth something." Inside, they continue to feel they're worth nothing.

3. Addiction can be a defense against boredom. Carl Jung called this a "drive to activity." You get hooked on "sensation," and your addiction provides a temporary but immediate high. Some studies show that compulsive shoppers and gamblers are "sensation seekers." They get an adrenaline rush in the thrill of the game or the high of the buy. Perhaps they feel understimulated in the rest of their lives, and so they see their addiction as the only way to feel "alive" and "powerful."

But calling what you feel a fear of boredom can also be misleading. Sometimes what you sense as boredom is actually a cover-up for all those feelings discussed above—feelings of boredom and apathy in your life are attempts at numbing yourself to negative emotions and shutting almost all feeling out of your life.

4. The effects of the addiction are consistent and predictable. You know that if you take a drink or a smoke or bring a new pair of earrings home, you can rely on feeling the same each time. Nakken calls this effect the "seductive part of addiction." Addiction causes you to experience a predictable mood change. In a chaotic world where people and events let you down, it's comforting to know that whenever you push your cash, check, or credit card across the counter, you are guaranteed to get something in return, whether it's an item or an experience. This comfort is illusory, however, because the immediate gratification that you experience costs you a high price in the long run.

5. Addiction offers short-term rewards that mask long-term harm. People persist in addictive behavior even though it inevitably results in harmful consequences. The harmful consequences can be physical, economic, and psychological. Harmful emotional consequences often follow close on the heels of the "high"—the addict recognizes the loss of control that led to the behavior and feels tremendous shame, guilt, and self-disgust. Nakken explains that addicts act on the emotional level of adolescents in that they live for the present moment without regard for even the immediate future. Part of disregarding the future is the ability to avoid looking at what you know to be a destructive, repetitive pattern. A vicious cycle ensues: the anxiety of this pattern may lead you right back to the supposed "relief" that the addictive behavior brings.

Cross-Addictions

Many psychologists have found evidence that those who report cross-addictions are often *cross-addicted* to other habits as well. Workaholics who abuse caffeine to keep them "up" often rely on alcohol to let them "down" at the end of the day. Those who abuse alcohol tend to smoke cigarettes; those who are heavy gamblers tend to be heavy drinkers, and so on. The National Council on Problem Gambling reports that in a 1984 study of affective disorders among pathological gamblers seeking treatment, 47 percent of compulsive gamblers in an inpatient treatment program were drug or alcohol abusers. Similar statistics are reported for such other addictions as eating disorders. Of course, it must be said that certain milieus—such as the gambling culture—encourage certain abuses, such as alcohol use. Environment certainly plays an important, if not crucial, part in encouraging addictions. Although you cannot choose the family into which you were born, you can certainly choose the people you want to be with and emulate in adulthood.

Where Differences Matter

So far, this chapter has highlighted the great similarities between addictions. These similarities offer promise in terms of treatment and support. But, as you know, there are crucial differences between addictions. It does matter whether you are chemically addicted to a substance or habitually addicted to an activity. It also matters whether the object of the addiction is something that can be cut out entirely—such as alcohol, drugs, and gambling—or whether it is in some measure a necessary part of life—such as eating and shopping.

In the latter case, when the addiction focuses on a normal life activity carried to an extreme, abstinence is clearly not an option. You simply can't never shop again—just as someone with an unhealthy relationship to food can't never eat again. Recovery involves redefining the relationship to the activity. It involves examining all the meanings the activity might represent and cutting out—or redirecting—the meanings that have nothing to do with the activity itself. It involves developing a clear self-awareness of the dimensions of the problem. Finally, recovery involves learning new, healthier approaches to the activity. This book is designed to guide you through this process and act as a support as you find a new balance.

The Smiled-Upon Addiction

Another crucial difference between addictions comes up with the subject of compulsive shopping. Mention alcoholism to someone, and you can expect to meet with sympathy and respect for the seriousness of the problem. (It wasn't always so—but AA has done a tremendous job of furthering awareness of the perils of alcoholism.) Mention compulsive shopping to someone, and chances are you will be greeted with smiles and even laughter. The media and vendors make light of the subject, with posters and T-shirts that say "Born to Shop," "He who has the most things when he dies, wins," "Veni, Vidi, Visa (I came, I saw, I shopped)," and "When the Going Gets Tough, the Tough Go Shopping." But there's nothing funny about being in debt up to your eyeballs, getting into constant fights about money, sneaking around hiding your purchases, and feeling that you might never manage your budget, your self-esteem, or your life.

Suffering from a "smiled-upon" addiction can be lonely. It can push your self-esteem even lower: how silly, you might think, to be so stressed out about something so frivolous. It can make it more difficult to admit you have a problem—since there's nothing like laughter to make light of a serious issue. And it can deprive you of crucial support during your recovery. Rest assured, though, that the problem is a grave one. Support groups formed to help compulsive shoppers have been flooded with phone calls. The topic has even made its way into academia, as researchers have begun to explore the personal and social forces that give rise to this growing problem. More papers are published on the subject of compulsive buying each year. Perhaps those who continue to scoff are simply avoiding too close a look at their own spending habits. They may laugh all the way into bankruptcy.

The Encouraged Addiction

It must be said that in this materialistic culture, shopping is encouraged. The more you buy, the healthier the economy—on the scale of macroeconomics, if not of your personal budget! Chapter 3 will explore many aspects of this culture, from advertising and marketing to architecture and philosophy. While a culture cannot make you shop, it does promote certain activities as positive and "cool." This cultural influence can be hard to see, but it is persuasive.

Think for a moment of the cigarette industry. For years, cigarettes were advertised not only as cool, but as *good for you*. Movie stars cut a slick image with their favorite brands, and teenagers followed suit. Women marked their independence by smoking proudly in public (this image continues today, in advertisements for one "lady's" brand of cigarettes). After the medical evidence was compiled, the Surgeon General issued a warning about smoking—two decades ago. Only now, however, is the social approval of smoking dimming. Teenagers continue to take up smoking, for the lasting image that it's cool persists in the media and the popular imagination. Society as a whole does not necessarily know what is good for you.

Alcoholics know something of the public pressure to drink. Alcohol is tied to associations of celebration and socialization and even to many religious and cultural ceremonies and traditions. But alcoholics have also organized and mobilized support units for themselves. They are assured, as soon as they admit that they are dependent on alcohol, that they are on the road to a healthier, happier lifestyle. The community of recovering alcoholics provides a mini-society of support and approval.

Compulsive shoppers cannot find this support so easily. Addressing a shopping problem often requires going against the grain of the values of the dominant culture. Have faith in your conviction that shopping is not always good for you. Be assured that you have the inner strength to support yourself through recovery. Be assured, also, that looking critically at your shopping behavior is most certainly a step toward a healthier, more balanced lifestyle. If you like, look around in your community for other compulsive shoppers— either through people you know, or perhaps a small advertisement in the local newspaper, or a twelve-step program such as Debtors Anonymous. There is strength in numbers.

The Problem and the Solution

It is our belief that compulsive shopping is a double-edged problem. On one hand, it is an addiction like many others, rooted in deep personal issues. The addictive behavior begins as an escape or a salve for the other problems and soon takes on a life of its own, becoming a new problem. Once this process has begun, the other side of the compulsive shopping problem sets in. Society fans and encourages the addiction, rather than calling it into question and making it difficult to pursue. (Most addictive drugs are illegal or controlled by prescription; alcohol use is restricted to adults.)

Given this model, our recovery plan for compulsive shopping also has two sides. The inner problem, addiction, must be recognized, measured, and confronted. Many of the chapters in this book focus on this process, offering exercises, plans, and support for what can be an enjoyable and liberating experience. At the same time, the outer problem, societal encouragement, must be recognized and questioned. No one is suggesting that society is your enemy—rather that society as a whole often promotes values that are not in your best interest as a healthy individual. Several chapters aim to give you a new perspective on these matters and help you see what is helpful and what is harmful in the world around you.

The intention of this book is not to dole out guilt, nor to scold you for your behavior, nor to leave you hanging your head in shame about your habit. Far from it! Rather, it is for you to become aware of how your problem affects your life and to realize that you have many options, all within your control. All that is asked is a willingness on your part to gain insight. Remember, it takes practice, perserverence, and commitment to make changes in your lifestyle. But think how dull and hopeless life would be if there were no possibilities for challenge, change, and growth.

If you suspect that you have a problem with overspending, but fear the seriousness of the word "addicted," allow yourself to relax at this very moment and put the word aside. There are many forms of addiction, and many ways that addiction is manifested in this society. Give yourself permission to explore the wide range of problem shopping behaviors you'll observe in this book and to compare them with your own experience. Opening yourself to the possibility of a problem is the first step toward self-awareness, recovery, and growth.

2

Are You a Compulsive Shopper?

"Typical" Profiles

At this point in exploring your shopping behavior, you may wonder what the "typical" compulsive shopper looks like. As it turns out, there is no typical problem shopper. Despite any stereotypes you may have heard, compulsive shoppers come from a wide range of backgrounds, encompass both sexes, and earn a wide range of incomes. They even have a wide range of spending patterns, including compulsive daily shopping, occasional binging, collecting, bargain hunting, buying multiples of each item, eternal TV-shopping, and many more variations. According to a 1991 article in the *New York Times*, an estimated 6 percent of the U.S. population has a problem with shopping and spending behaviors. That's a whopping 15 million people. No wonder the people and the problem come in all shapes and sizes!

That said, there are some behavioral similarities you may find interesting. By far the most common symptom of problem shoppers is *low self-esteem*. A compulsive shopper may think that strength and beauty can only be brought in from the outside; he or she can then get caught in a downward self-esteem spiral by returning home with too many purchases and feeling even worse about being "out-of-control." Many compulsive shoppers feel a related *sense of emptiness*, a nagging feeling that they have to keep searching for something that will fill a void within them.

Not that compulsive shoppers focus exclusively on themselves. Another common feature among compulsive shoppers is the great deal of time and energy they spend *thinking about other people*, and trying to please them. Here again a key element is the need to look outside for validation and support. Still, compulsive shoppers can be very *generous*. The problem comes when they begin to confuse material gifts with love and the pleasant reactions of salespeople with genuine friendship.

In a surprising twist, many compulsive shoppers enjoy particularly *high-risk behaviors*. One woman in a compulsive shopping support group described speeding in her car as a favorite release: several members of the group agreed. Two out of the ten people in the same group said they went parachute jumping regularly! Of course, running up a substantial credit card debt is a form of risk. Researchers posit that compulsive spenders might have low levels of a particular body chemical produced by excitement or stimulation; if so, they need to arrange their lives to create the excitement that will generate the chemical. Also, compulsive shoppers on average have a keen *ability to fantasize*. Stepping into a glittering showroom, they easily project themselves into the unreal tableau, no matter how inappropriate it is for their lifestyles, needs, or incomes. They also forget the connection between the money they charge and the money they have available to pay.

Finally, many compulsive shoppers have *a vague sense that the problem goes back to childhood*. Perhaps they remember having strict limits imposed on their budgets or lifestyles, or perhaps they recall fights between their parents about money, or they may even feel that money was used to demonstrate love at home. The important point is the *feeling* that the problem is deep-rooted. On average, too, compulsive shoppers have an unusual *tendency towards anxiety and depression*. Whether this tendency comes before or after the growth of the shopping and debt problem is open to debate.

These traits form only a rough outline of anyone's shopping behavior. You alone know the true shape and size of your shopping problem—even if you don't always admit or even recognize it. Throughout the course of this chapter, you will have a chance to sort through what you know about your behavior.

A Few Good Reasons to Shop— His and Hers

It's a common stereotype to think of women as the real shoppers. Indeed, women are more often socialized to shop, in part to fulfill their traditional role of taking care of the home and the children's needs, but also to conform to other patterns of expected behavior— for example, "blowing off steam" by going out with friends and spending money (stereotypically, someone else's). In fact, experts believe that men may be as susceptible to problem shopping behavior as women. Men may not talk about it as much or even admit or recognize the problem. But, as you'll see, the social forces that can drive women to shop can exert just as strong a pull on men—if in different forms.

Women: A Quest for Validation and Recognition

Women have traditionally had far fewer outlets for self-exploration (and escape) outside the home than men. This situation is changing, but old habits die hard. Shopping filled the void when women were housebound with children, and shopping continues to do so for many women, whether inside the house or out.

The traditional shoppers. In advertisements and the popular imagination, women are portrayed as the shoppers of the family and are celebrated for shopping wisely. Their well-decorated houses are admired by neighbors and mothers-in-law; their well-chosen clothes are approved of by friends and strangers; their healthy food choices keep the family happy. A woman proves her taste, status, and even intelligence and care through the objects she buys and provides for her family. Thus, shopping is one of the few areas of traditional validation for women.

Quest for beauty and status. Women who shop compulsively tend to binge on such items as clothing, jewelry, and makeup. Interestingly, these are all items that serve to mark a woman's beauty and status. No matter how accomplished a woman is in this society, she can still feel judged on the basis of her external appearance. Perceiving a lack of respect or status—that is, positive feedback about her character and achievements—many women struggle to improve their image in the external terms that society consistently rewards.

Rare indulgence. Psychologists often state that women are more prone to self-sacrifice than men. The basic fact of pregnancy means giving up control of one's own body for a time. Motherhood involves placing one's children's welfare above one's own. Little wonder that women become frustrated with this role even as they treasure its rewards. Shopping can be one forum where a woman takes care of her own needs, however she sees fit. Whether she works outside the home or not, her impression that she gives more than she takes and works hard for all she has can lead to an understandable urge for self-indulgence. Unfortunately, material rewards may come to seem the only form of self-indulgence available, or even desirable, after a shopping habit is formed.

The social network. Studies have consistently shown that women are much more likely to look to their network of family and friends for support and even identity than men are. Shopping can be a means of social interaction and connection to the world. For some women, shopping is an ideal activity to share with a friend. For others, the salespeople who populate stores become friends. Either way, a shopping mall can seem like a microcosm of the outside world, and shopping a sign of participation in it.

Proof of love and friendship. Because social relations are so important to women, many look for "proof" of their bonds of love and friendship. All too often, this proof takes on material form. A woman may develop the habit of shopping for random gifts for other people to demonstrate her continued affection. She may also begin to shower herself with gifts as a tangible sign of self-acceptance and love or as a rare break from the self-hatred and insecurity she may feel. Shopping can begin to stand for or even replace love.

Power. The moment of purchase may be one of the few traditional moments of power for women. When women earned no money, they exercised financial power through choosing where to direct their husband's funds. Now that women have grown used to bringing home their own paychecks, the moment of paying can allow women to demonstrate (and celebrate) their hard-earned wealth. This culture offers relatively few experiences of power to most women; signing a charge slip can be a momentary brush with the strength and status denied elsewhere.

Men: Collectors and Experts

You may not think it's "cool" for men to shop. This stereotypical image persists, despite a booming consumer industry aimed specifically at men. Believe it or not, men get themselves into as much trouble as women through shopping. The fact that it isn't cool, however, leads to some special problems.

For one thing, few men are willing to admit they may have a problem shopping—and fewer still may be willing to do anything about it. The director of one recovery program for compulsive spenders in San Francisco said that *half* the phone calls received at the program are from men. Only about 10 percent of these men actually follow through and get help, however. Men who shop compulsively may feel additional guilt because of this silence and perceived stigma.

Of course, there are tricks to describing the problem that make it all seem better. One way to describe a compulsive purchaser of certain items is a *collector*: now there's a respectable word. Collectors of model trains, wines, stamps, coins, historical memorabilia, books, tools, and so on are not necessarily compulsive. But collecting is a hobby built around purchase, and many collectors get themselves in over their heads, finding that they cannot stop. Attending conventions, subscribing to catalogs, pursuing the "right tool": all can lead to financial and shopping disaster. Be aware that compulsive shopping in men may be lurking behind different euphemistic terms: expert, fanatic, connoisseur, enthusiast, fiend, hobbyist, nut, and so on.

That said, what are the forces that might drive men to shop?

Symbols of wealth and success. The pressure has always been on men to succeed and to provide. As Thorstein Veblen noted a century ago, who'll know you've succeeded if you don't put it on display? (Veblen coined the term "conspicuous consumption" to describe this phenomenon.) Big-ticket items such as cars and fancy stereo and photographic equipment announce to the world the wealth and status of the man who owns them. Because men go for big-ticket items, they can spend exorbitantly without feeling as if they're spending any significant *time* shopping. That's not the bottom line that counts in this case, though.

Symbols of leisure. Far better than money from a paycheck is money in the bank and the time to spend it. The upper class has always indulged in "conspicuous leisure," as Veblen also noted. It follows, then, that those who wish to appear successful will cultivate the habits of a life of ease. Hobbies are one wonderful way to do this. Investing in fancy outdoor equipment, or restoring vintage cars, or developing an extensive CD collection announces to the world that you not only have the money for these pursuits, but have the time to build and enjoy them. Once secured in the equipment of the hobby, the temptation remains to keep upgrading one's equipment to remain "serious" and on the "cutting edge." All of which can keep the credit bill mounting.

Rewards for work. Most men continue to spend most of their time working. If they fill a traditional role and work to provide for a wife and children, they may feel they're due for a personal reward. Even if husband and wife both work, a man will feel as entitled as a woman to some personal compensation. "Why work so hard to earn it if I can't spend it?" the reasoning might go. In this way, spending is made to seem the reward for the hard work. In a pattern similar to women who overspend, a lack of spending can begin to feel like deprivation and punishment.

Instant personality. Just as a woman feels pressure from movies, ads, and stereotypes to look beautiful, a man feels pressure to seem fascinating or strong or bold and daring. One quick way to fill these pressures is through purchase. A car in particular seems to many people the extension of the driver's personality: sudden sexiness or upper-class tastes or macho strength all seem available with a single purchase. A hobby can add instant spice to a man's personality and welcome him into whatever group or society shares that hobby. You too can be a rare book collector or a sporty rake in a red convertible. Your credit card will suffer, though!

Shopping Danger Signals

How can you find your way around this maze of behaviors and forces? Below are three brief diagnostic exercises. Don't worry about your ratings or your "scores"—these are for your eyes only. Of course, it's in your best interest to be as honest as possible.

1. How You Feel About Shopping

One way to diagnose the severity of your shopping habit is to think about how you feel about shopping. Do any of these traits sound familiar to you? Check the ones that do.

☐ I feel a lack of control over my spending habits.

☐ I feel guilty when I shop.

☐ I don't know—or want to admit—how much I shop.

☐ I tend to hide purchases and shopping expeditions from my loved ones.

☐ Shopping is my favorite method of relieving tension and anxiety.

☐ I often care more about the action of buying than what I actually buy.

☐ My closet is full of unused things.

☐ I often buy things I can't afford.

☐ Other people would be horrified if they knew how much I shopped.

☐ I buy myself things to make myself feel better.

Each of these statements is a shopping danger signal, reported by people who have admitted to problem shopping. The list was developed by professors Thomas O'Guinn and Ronald Faber, researchers in the field of compulsive shopping, and reported in a *New York Times* article on the subject. There's no way to "score" this little self-test. The more statements you checked, the more work you may have to do.

2. The Purpose of the Purchase

Another way to think about your shopping behavior is to ponder the purpose of the majority of your purchases. In the first column below, list your five most recent purchases.

Most Recent Purchase   Assign a Reason

1._____   _____

2._____   _____

3._____   _____

4._____   _____

5._____   _____

Now, use the list that follows to recall why you bought each one. Put the number of the reason that comes closest to capturing your thoughts about each purchase in the right-hand column.

1. A pick-me-up

2. Something I needed and set out to buy

3. Impulse gift for someone

4. Necessary gift for someone

5. I deserve it (even if I can't afford it)

6. I deserve it (and I can afford it)

7. There was extra money in my wallet

8. Specific item to improve home

9. To fill time

10. To replace something worn or broken

11. To please (or annoy) someone

12. To match an incomplete outfit or set

13. I don't know

14. "Necessary" reason not listed:_____

15. "Irrational" reason not listed:_____

Be honest as you rate your list—no one need see it but you. Once you're satisfied that you've come close to capturing your reasons for each purchase, look over the numbers you filled in. *Even* numbers represent reasons that everyone uses to shop; these are cases where shopping is essential and appropriate. *Odd* numbers represent reasons that don't make immediate rational sense. Which do you see more often on your list?

3. How You Use Your Purchases

Finally, ask yourself how often you have used each of the five purchases you listed earlier. Assign a number to each one:

1. Constantly   Purchase 1: _____

2. Often   Purchase 2: _____

3. Occasionally   Purchase 3: _____

4. Once   Purchase 4: _____

5. Never   Purchase 5: _____

Look over your numbers. Take an average (add them up and divide by 5) and see where you fall. If your average is 3.5 or greater, chances are the moment of purchase is more important to you than the item purchased. If your average is 3 or lower, the items purchased are particularly important to you. Most compulsive shoppers will have an average on the high end of the scale.

Shopping Continuum

Perhaps you confirmed your suspicions above that you really do have a shopping problem. Perhaps you think it's not as bad as you thought. Perhaps you feel overwhelmed and scared. A good step to take right now is to give yourself an overview of the problem. Problem shopping falls along a wide range of behaviors. The scale that follows can help you see where you fall.

Hates to shop	Subsistence shopping	Recreational shopping	Excessive shopping	Addicted shopping
Avoids shopping; borrows, mends, and goes without.	Shops only when absolutely necessary; plans purchases carefully.	Occasionally splurges; can window-shop for hours without purchase.	Shops on a frequent, regular basis; follows a strenuous shopping "regimen."	Fears cannot get by without regular doses of shopping.
Saves compulsively.	Budgets money for necessities, saves.	Splurges when there is extra cash...may exceed own preset limits.	Avoids managing money...may be shocked when bills come.	Panic/denial about money issues...aware of being "out of control."

Hates to shop. Persons on this end of the continuum avoid shopping "at all cost." They are save-aholics who find very little, if any, enjoyment in walking through a mall, trying things on, or buying something. If they have to shop, they very quickly become impatient. They tend to purchase the first thing they see that meets their needs so that they can get out of there. They will make do with old clothes and other recycled items so that they won't have to go through the onerous experience of shopping. These people simply cannot understand what turns anyone on about shopping. Money in the bank seems far more exciting to them.

Subsistence and recreational shopping. These persons will occasionally splurge when they think they can afford it. They usually save up for an item so that they don't have to put the expense on a credit card. If they do put it on a card, they tend to pay it all when the first bill comes. They plan well ahead for their purchase and comparison-shop to get the best deal. They are patient and willing to wait until the best deal comes along. Subsistence shoppers can take or leave the experience of shopping—it simply doesn't matter to them one way or the other. They are very practical about shopping and about their purchases. Recreational shoppers can window-shop for hours without feeling the need to make a purchase. Shopping provides an occasional diversion, a change of pace, and an opportunity to socialize with friends. Shopping for both these groups is on a no-pressure basis. Occasionally they may exceed their own preset limits, but that doesn't happen very often.

Excessive shopping. Tending toward the compulsive side of the continuum, these persons are drawn to the experience of shopping. They shop on a frequent, regular basis and are prone to impulse buys. They begin to rationalize purchasing something whether they can afford it or not. The "item" becomes more important than their budget, and they tend to throw self-discipline and any personal goals out the window when they are tempted to spend. Shopping is an important part of their weekly or daily lives. Excessive shoppers may not be in deep financial difficulty as a result of their habit, but they routinely spend enough to feel twinges of guilt. They tend to avoid managing money and may be "shocked" when the bills come.

Addicted shopping. On the far end of the continuum, these persons experience deep financial difficulty as a result of their spending habits. They are simply out of control, with multiple credit cards charged to the limit, bad credit ratings, and zero cash flow. They are likely to have marital and family conflicts as a result. Their emotions may spring in two entirely different directions: (1) Either they feel deeply ashamed and guilty of their habit but powerless over it, or (2) they completely deny that their habit is connected to anything else, such as their emotional state or families of origin.

These simplified groupings may look to you at first as though they overgeneralize the wide range of spending behaviors available to compulsive shoppers. However, the scale serves two purposes. First, it helps you get started. When problems loom large, they may feel overwhelming at first, paralyzing you into inaction. You don't know where to begin, so you don't begin at all, hoping that some miracle will happen (perhaps you'll win the lottery?) to get you off the hook. Second, the scale gives you a sense of proportion. Perhaps you feel so embarrassed by your problem that you tend to magnify it, making it worse than it really is. Or perhaps you tend to deny your problem, looking the other way and hoping it will disappear. Either way, this quick behavioral assessment prepares you for this book's journey through an inquiry into your own situation.

How Much Is Too Much?

Since shoppers have such a wide variety of stories, any measure of excess has to be relative. After all, someone earning $12,000 a year who loves to buy herself jewelry from crafts fairs may be just fine. Someone earning $120,000 a year who stops at every sidewalk vendor she passes to buy jewelry and scarves and hair clips may have a problem.

A good way to look at excessive shopping habits is by percentage. When you shop you spend more than just money—you spend time and energy, too. Here is your chance to consider how much of each of these resources you spend on your shopping habits. You want some of each left over for every other area of your life, after all!

Shopping as a Percentage of Your Income

Credit experts say that any debt beyond 20 percent of your take-home pay is dangerous. Let's say you earn $30,000, and pay $10,000 in taxes, rent, and utilities. Your take-home pay is $20,000. If you owe more than 20 percent of this amount, or more than $4,000, you face credit trouble. This formula is simplified, but it gives you a ballpark idea.

What does credit trouble mean? On a basic level, it means you will not be able to pay your debt back in a timely fashion. Paying your minimum balances will continue to service your debt, but only barely reduce the balance.

In a worst-case scenario, you may face personal bankruptcy. The number of Americans claiming personal bankruptcy has been climbing steadily over the past few years, jumping 152 percent from 1984 (with 285,000) to 1990 (718,000), according to a recent *New York Times* article. From 1989 to 1990 alone, the number increased 16.4 percent from the previous year. There is no indication that this trend is slowing down.

There are many alternatives to bankruptcy, and chances are good that you won't have to face such a drastic solution. Wise budgeting and debt restructuring can help you pull out of almost any money trouble you find yourself in (chapter 10 will get you started). But the best way to avoid trouble is preventive maintenance. Think about your level of debt next to your level of income. Does it seem problematic to you?

Rough worksheet:

(Figure per month or per year)

My approximate debt: _____

My approximate net income (after taxes):   _____

Percentage of debt to income: _____ %

Shopping as a Percentage of Your Time

According to one therapist who treats compulsive shoppers, if shopping is the high point of your day, you've got a problem. This skews the story a bit. True, there are some shoppers who plan each day around shopping. But there are also some who abstain for weeks or even months at a time, only to "lose it" in the wild frenzy of a shopping binge. Both types may still lose valuable chunks of time to his or her habit.

If shopping is a necessary part of every day, it takes on meaning far beyond the actual errand. Shopping becomes sewn into your daily routine, and changing that habit can feel like rip-ping the very fabric of your life. It can be done, however. Indeed, many shoppers feel that they discover a treasure-trove of time when they begin to cut down on shopping—time to spend on more productive pursuits.

An alternative problem is shopping every day to fill a void of boredom. In this case, it helps to remember how much you *pay* to fill that void. For the same price (or probably far less), a dance or crafts class or the purchase of a musical instrument can fill the void more productively. Indeed, for a far lower price a volunteer position or a job might work. The key is to find an activity you enjoy with a more lasting and fulfilling purpose than shopping.

Shopping as a Percentage of Your Energy

You spend energy running around the mall. Carrying packages from the store to the car and into your house requires reasonably strong biceps and quadriceps. How many calories do you suppose you burn just by reaching into your purse for your wallet and snapping it open? No doubt about it, shopping can be exhausting (and exhilarating, most compulsive shoppers would insist).

The real energy expenditure for compulsive shoppers comes in terms of worry. Planning shopping errands might be fun, but facing the music after a shopping binge is emotionally draining. Facing angry creditors is frightening; facing your own dwindling bankbook or angry spouse is humiliating. When shopping habits involve lying about and hiding purchases, the mental, physical, and emotional toll goes up. Even denying the existence of the problem to yourself requires tremendous psychic energy.

Cutting back on your shopping habit requires commitment and energy, but once you calculate how much is already spent in every phase of maintaining that habit, you may well find you have energy to divert to other areas of your life. That surplus gives you a chance to work on lasting, rather than fleeting, rewards.

Worksheet: Time and Energy Pie

To get an idea of the relative time and energy you devote to shopping, consider the "pie" below. The entire pie represents a 24-hour day, which is yours to cut up.

Begin by shading in the time you spend sleeping. For most people, this will be about one-third of the pie.

Next, shade in the amount of time you spend working on a typical weekday. If you work outside the home, include commuting. Again, for most people this will be about one-third of the pie or more.

What's left, after you've marked out time for working and sleeping, is your disposable time. But wait—it's not free leisure time yet.

Shade in the amount of time you spend eating. Include meal preparation and cleanup time too. Three hours would represent one-eighth of the pie, for instance.

Shade in the amount of time you spend doing regular chores: walking the dog, cleaning the house, driving the kids around, whatever keeps your daily life running smoothly.

Now, take a look at the remaining wedge. This is your truly free time. Ask yourself how much of *that* wedge is taken up by shopping? (Other options are hobbies, relaxation, reading, going to cultural events, walking, meeting friends, and so on.) If you find that most of your free wedge goes to shopping, chances are that shopping is eating up too much of your life's pie!

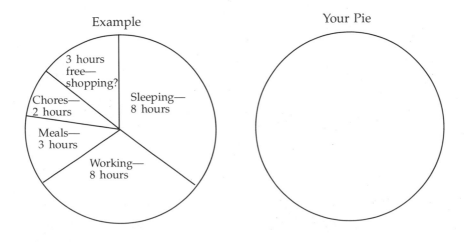

Example

3 hours free— shopping?

Chores— 2 hours

Meals— 3 hours

Sleeping— 8 hours

Working— 8 hours

Your Pie

Appraising Your Style

As these first two chapters have demonstrated, no two people are exactly alike in their spending patterns—family influences, cultural trends, and simple habits vary from individual to individual. And no objective measure can neatly and precisely determine who fits or doesn't fit into the category of "compulsive shopper." Compulsive shoppers come from different walks of life, genders, races, and income levels. Their motivations to spend are diverse and culturally complicated. But all share in some behavioral similarities, and these can shed light on your style of compulsive shopping.

Given the wide range of possible behaviors and motivations, your best bet is to appraise your style honestly. Where do you fall on the various continuums and scales in this chapter? What underlying motives are you aware of now? Which habits do you feel you have control over and which feel overwhelming to you? Rest assured, if shopping interferes with your life, health, and finances, and overall well-being (and you know it deep down when it does), then changing your shopping behaviors can have a positive impact on all of these areas.

3

How Our Culture Helps You Shop

"To gain and hold the esteem of men," wrote Thorstein Veblen a century ago, "it is not sufficient merely to possess wealth or power. The wealth or power must be put in evidence." No shopping scholar could put it better today. Who'll respect you for your taste or your wealth if they can't see it in the shape of a designer suit? Showing your finery in public is a way of demonstrating your wealth and power (and taste and personality) to all the strangers and friends you encounter in a modern city day—or on a typical stroll through the mall. It takes less time for people to judge you for what they see you *have* than it takes for them to stop and ask you what you *do*. Much less than for them to ask you who you *are*.

Of course, you care about more than what other people think of you. It's what you think about yourself that really matters. The danger, however, is that you yourself come to believe in these material signs of identity. You begin to confuse image (how other people see you) with self-image (how you see yourself). You begin to confuse self-image with self-worth. Ultimately you may think you are only as good as the car you drive or your newest pair of shoes.

In this chapter, you'll have a chance to examine this state of affairs. A culture cannot make you shop or force you to accept a certain view of things. But cultural values are like the air you breathe. They surround you and sustain you and influence you no matter how invisible they may seem. In the following sections, you'll learn to see this air and begin to identify which components nurture you and which may be hazardous to your health.

The first section explores materialism, the dominant trait of American culture today. You might see this as a philosophical approach to shopping. What does it mean when people confuse who you are with what you have?

Section two takes a look at the advertising industry and the many ways it affects you and your view of the world. By asking "What's wrong with this picture?" you'll begin to build a healthy distance between that glossy, impossible ad-world and the real world you live in.

Section three introduces you to marketing science: the other side of the advertising image. The marketing industry that informs advertisers is growing more sophisticated by the day, and you may be surprised by some of the cutting-edge techniques for subliminal selling. Two new waves of marketing deserve your special attention. One is called "psychographics"—a new and improved version of demographic questioning. The second is the shift to experiential shopping—the study of what really lures you into the stores. Like designers of an advanced virtual reality game, marketers weave music and aroma and stage design and more to create an unreal but all-inclusive world, into which you step and suspend your disbelief—at your own peril.

Section four offers some ideas for thinking about healthier modes of behavior for yourself.

Keep in mind that parts of this chapter may be difficult to accept. Advertisers can feel like old, trusted friends. Going down to the mall can be an enjoyable and important release for you. No

one is suggesting that these resources aren't powerful: th...
reason they speak to you so intimately and persuasively. I
the length of this chapter, allow yourself to consider the poss... ...ty
that it may not all be in your best interest.

A Material World

Think of the phrase "She's got it all." It spells success. Of course,
it only spells success as measured by possessions. In a material
world, though, that is precisely how success is measured. You are
what you have. Successful people have more things, and better
things. If you've "made it," you have it all.

This message is pervasive in modern society. Stories about
rich and famous people abound, forever linking the words of
"rich" and "famous": the connection seems natural, as if either one
leads to the other as a matter of course. Success stories detail the
trappings of wealth: cars, houses, toys, parties, art. People who do
the most boring things imaginable become instant celebrities for
their wealth. They become "somebodies."

Of course, the rich have always been with us, but in other
eras people were also celebrated for their accomplishments. Heroes
were often warriors or explorers or inventors. Now creators of fantasy are the big stars—pop musicians and movie actors, for instance—and even athletes are better known for their salaries than
their throwing arms. But this perception of things doesn't pertain
exclusively to the rich and famous. Someone who drives a big,
boxy car is seen as domestic and family-oriented. Somebody who
drives a little sports car is racy and sexy. Someone who drives a
wreck is shabby. Think of all the judgments you make about people
before you even know their names or how they spend their days.

And so, knowing you'll be recognized and typed by your
possessions, you turn your attention to acquiring the things that
will reflect the appropriate identity-message. Shopping becomes a
means of self-expression and self-definition—you begin to search
for items that are really "you." It takes more than one item to do
this, of course. As writers Mary Douglas and Baron Isherwood put
it, thinking that a single item can represent the fully complex you

is like thinking that a single word from a poem can represent the full meaning of the poem.

Shopping in this society becomes a self-defining task and a never-ending task. As you begin to change and grow, after all, your cache of possessions has to change and grow with you. How else will people know you've changed? And so you keep shopping. This is just one angle of the pressure a materialistic society gives you to buy and to buy more and to just keep buying.

But a deeper danger comes from focusing on the surface of things. Instead of buying a pair of shoes to reflect your sense of style, you start to look to your shoes to *provide* your style. This line of thinking puts your identity in peril every time you dress: "I can't find those pearls! I'm incomplete!" If your mountain bicycle or anything else precious is stolen, you may feel you've lost a part of yourself. Here's one man's description of the magical effect his new Porsche had on him (as published in the *Wall Street Journal*, 1985, and quoted by consumer researcher Russell Belk in 1988).

> Sometimes I test myself. We have an ancient, battered Peugeot, and I drive it for a week. It rarely breaks, and it gets great mileage. But when I pull up next to a beautiful woman, I am still the geek with the glasses.
>
> Then I get back into the Porsche. It roars and tugs to get moving. It accelerates even going uphill at 80. It leadeth trashy women...to make pouting looks at me at stoplights. It makes me feel like a tomcat on the prowl....
>
> Nothing else in my life compares—except driving along Sunset at night in the 928, with the sodium-vapor lamps reflecting off the wine-red finish, with the air inside reeking of tan glove-leather upholstery and the...Blaupunkt playing the Shirelles so loud it makes my hair vibrate. And with the girls I will never see again pulling up next to me, giving the car a once-over, and looking at me as if I were a cool guy, not a worried, over-extended 40-year-old schnook writer.

Imagine how he'd feel if this adjunct of himself were sma: or stolen—as if a part of himself were bruised, as if his sex appeal had vanished with a poof. The less secure you are with yourself, the more you look to your things to provide your sense of self.

Are You What You Have?

A consumer researcher named Russell Belk came up with the term "extended self" to describe this inclusive sense of identity, where one's possessions—and physical self and ideas and even family members—are incorporated into one's self-image and self-understanding. You may lose track of the dividing line between what's you and what's yours.

Think about it. Why are people so keen to collect old possessions of their idols—Elvis's guitar, or James Dean's socks? Perhaps because they see those objects as representing an actual piece of the idol, of that person's extended self. When people collect items from people or cultures they know nothing about, they may want to associate themselves with certain virtues or values they perceive that culture to represent—the refinement of old English furniture, perhaps, or the exotic quality of antique Chinese coins. The hope is that some of it will rub off from the item to them, and become part of their own extended self. That's what the French sociologist Claude Levi Strauss suggested.

People love Elvis because of what he did and who he was, not because of what he *had*. The same is true of James Dean— although, to be fair, the leather jacket helped! But once again a switch happens; you see what the idol has, begin to confuse this with the idol's personality, and want to have the same material things in order to come closer to the idol's personal magic. Picture hordes of teenage girls dressing like a sultry pop-star; they want her sense of cool, her rebellious, provocative, and independent style. Few of them *sing* to achieve this; they follow society's focus on having, rather than doing, and buy the same earrings and leather jackets she wears. Little boys want to have superhero capes more than they want to fight crime.

Alas, chances are that those teenage girls and little boys find only momentary pleasure in their new acquisitions. The leather jackets certainly make the girls look cooler, but it's doubtful they'll find fame, fortune, and artistic fulfillment through them. The very next season they will probably need something new to feel invigorated, just as the little boys switch over to Teenage Mutant Ninja Turtle lunch boxes. One philosopher of Western society predicted this pattern of dissatisfaction: Karl Marx.

The False Path to Happiness

Marx wrote that, within a commodity world, "*all* the physical and spiritual senses are replaced by the sense of *having*." But having, he cautioned, is the false path to happiness. A "fetishism of commodities" takes over, in which the social relationships between people are eclipsed or overtaken by the economic relationships between commodities. The happiness that individuals once sought in themselves and in each other is replaced by a thing, a product. Happiness always seems one purchase away—and thus becomes unattainable.

According to Marx, the true path to happiness is not having, but *doing*. By doing—that is, working or creating—one has a chance at finding meaning in existence and pride in oneself. That's the gist of Marx's critique of capitalism: when workers no longer control the fruits of their labor, they are stripped of identity and purpose. An even more extreme view is suggested by psychologist Erich Fromm, who said that for true happiness, one should think not about having and not even about doing, but simply about *being*. A focus on being allows complete and immediate satisfaction—after all, simply by existing you're a success. This approach frees you to give, share, and sacrifice to society however you like, without risking harm to your identity.

But it's hard to live in an objectless world of the spirit when material comforts beckon from every side. Indeed, isn't this part of the miracle of modern America? More of us have more things than anywhere else in the world. Goods are plentiful and *accessible*. This is, after all, the reward of a successful free market economy. Just by living in America, we feel entitled to a large cache of sparkling treasures—or at least new cars, big houses, and ever-updated fashions.

A look around, however, suggests that Marx may have had a point. As a nation, the more things we have, the more things we want. Satisfaction is not part of the program. Where did this insatiable desire come from? In part, you might say, it's human nature to want more. But in part—and this is the part you can do something about—the collective demand for more and more things is a deliberate outgrowth of modern business. Everywhere you go, you, as a good American consumer, are instructed to want and to keep wanting more.

An Introduction to Advertising

Between 1200 and 1500 new products appear on American shelves each year. If no one buys them, enormous investments are wasted. And so most new products appear in a shower of publicity, accompanied by a parade of advertisements, and an all-out effort to convince you that you've been waiting for this product all your life. It's an axiom of advertising that a company creates the demand for its product. If a consumer is curious about a product, he or she may buy it once. If a consumer *needs* a product, he or she will buy it again and again. You can see which approach makes better business sense. And you can see why you see, hear, and feel advertising almost everywhere you go.

You're aware and you're not aware of the advertising surrounding you. Some advertising, of course, goes for the gut response. No one told you you needed Oscar Meyer Weiners when you were a kid: they sang it to you. Memories of childhood jingles last throughout life, leaving you whistling "I'm an Oscar Meyer Weiner" when you least expect it and telling you something of the powerful effect of music. Walking down any city street, you're confronted with dozens of logos and brand names that you recognize and take in without even consciously noticing them. The subliminal effect of such techniques can be powerful. But the serious sell of products comes through an appeal to your sense of need.

Now, consumers aren't stupid. It would be hard for a company to convince you that you've made it this far in life with a severe handicap because you haven't had their new scarf ring or ceiling fan or lemon drop. After all, most new products are either subtle variations of old ones or so new that it hasn't occurred to anyone to want such a thing before. But that doesn't mean you don't have unfilled needs. Think on a larger scale. Chances are you've always wanted to belong and to succeed and to look beautiful. You've always needed love and warmth and friendship. These are the needs, everlasting and never completely filled, that advertisers have learned to latch on to. The most powerful advertising aims to convince you that a material product will fill your highest, most spiritual needs.

A lemon drop is liable to be sold as health and joy, not a lump of sugar. A face cream is sold as youth and beauty, not deionized water and mineral oil. And a soft drink is sold as a ticket to belonging: think of all those happy people singing "I'm a Pepper, too," or "Join the Pepsi generation." Look at most ads, and you'll realize that you're asked to respond to something more profound than information about the product. You'll see tremendous promise for some *feeling* you want—and, if you're to believe the ad, it's a feeling you can buy. You might feel good just watching or listening to the ad. And what's wrong with that? Indeed, the world might be a nicer place if more people sounded so excited and concerned about your happiness and health.

But if ads pick up on your biggest hopes, they also pick up on your greatest fears. Remember the ad "A sprinkle a day helps keep odor away"? A car-full of disgusted commuters sang this to an isolated offender in the front seat—mocking him for the crime of smelling like himself (first thing in the morning, too, hardly the right time to perspire!) instead of like the company's baby powder. The result: social isolation and humiliation. The advertising of one well-known mouthwash in the 1930s coined the word "halitosis," a pseudo-scientific word to describe bad breath. They ran enormous portraits of healthy, successful looking people for whom something had gone terribly wrong: "Case study number 317: Career advancement blocked," or "Social hopes dashed." The company made a disease of a problem everyone has at some time or another. These scare tactics continue today. Mothers-in-law check glassware for waterspots, while cute school girls in the second row check potential dates for dandruff. The message here is not "our product will make you belong," but "*not* using our product will keep you apart."

Is there lasting harm in any of this? After all, you know these are just advertisements. Sometimes you want their products. Sometimes they give you cute jingles to sing along to. Most look nice: one writer uses the phrase "Alice in Wonderland" to describe that sparkling fantasy world you want to step right into. Some are just plain entertaining or funny. But even as you laugh at ads, they slowly chip away at your defenses. They get under your skin; that's the magic behind the jingle. (Did any from your childhood come to mind?) They hit on powerful desires and fears. Ultimately, they suggest a framework for looking at the world around you and at yourself.

What's Wrong with This Picture?

Too shiny. Look at car ads, and you'll almost never see guard rails, lane markings, or street lights on the twisting highway—all these suggest limits, the opposite of what the car company wants you to think about. In many ads, cars are left with their headlights on and doors open, perhaps parked by a waterfront view of a big city skyline, with the owners chatting nearby in full evening dress on a mysteriously shiny floor (an outdoor showroom?). In the real world, they'd be mugged and the car stolen before the lady could remove one of her stiletto heels. As in the stores themselves, there is a glittering, always-perfect, always-happy polish to everything and everyone involved in the scene around the product. When you look up from that magazine ad, of course your hair looks sloppy by comparison. Chances are your friends look boring too, since you can't remember the last time one of them met a male model in a ballroom and showed up in just her Maidenform bra.

Too insatiable. What good would an ad do that emphasized joy in what you already have or what you do or who you are? Relatively little, unless it suggested that the product was an essential part of it. Instead, ads encourage you to ponder what you need, what you want, and what you lack. Even if these desires are for spiritual values—wanting love or respect—ads channel them back towards things. The strength and virtue you crave have to be brought in—bought in—from the outside, not developed from within.

Too competitive. Actors in commercials earn the esteem and envy of their neighbors by driving up in brand new, expensive-looking cars. The message is that respect is bought by purchase, by fancy material things—not by, say, working hard (that would mean dirt!) or being generous. The sub-message is that earning the esteem and envy of the neighbors is valuable: it's a competitive world, and success is measured by visible things. Indeed, the advertisement may well go on to announce that the car is available at a never-before-heard-of low rate, so that you can appear to be more financially successful in the eyes of your neighbors than you actually are. It's the appearance in your neighbors' eyes that counts, the ad suggests.

Too envious. Most ads work by arousing envy—viewers want to be more like the models they see in the ad. The people in the ad always seem to be having tremendous fun. They look healthy, relaxed, and perfectly successful and glad. An art critic named John Berger has suggested that the real source of envy people feel for such images of perfection is envy towards *themselves*. The ad shows people a version of themselves that might be—a more successful, happier, healthier version. The magical transformation takes place after buying or using the product in the ad. Viewers become dissatisfied with their present selves and pin their hopes on a tomorrow and a self that is dependent on the product.

Too patronizing. Think of the ad "You've come a long way, baby," for Virginia Slims cigarettes. The ad picks up on a woman's belief or hope or pride that she has more freedom and choice than she did a century ago. By validating a woman's wish for equal rights, the ad taps strong emotions. It even uses the language of the women's rights movement, insisting that women have "freedom of choice." Those emotions are then channeled into...a *cigarette*, as if that one product were the tangible proof of progress. Never mind that women have long fought for rights as a means of taking better care of themselves. The ad implies that women have come to enjoy all they wanted and that cigarettes are the symbol and the reward for their struggle. (As if the cigarette company cares primarily about women's welfare!) Think, too, of the commercial "This Bud's for all you do," aimed at blue-collar working men. These men tend to feel underappreciated for their hard work in society, and so the ad strives to validate their sense that they do plenty and deserve recognition. Their joy and relief at being recognized are channeled into...*beer*. Each ad validates the viewer's sense that more is deserved—and offers as reward a medically harmful product. The ad may feel good to watch, but in the end it clouds perceptions and defuses emotions that are far from resolved.

Too superficial. All ads, by definition, emphasize *having*. They emphasize *doing* only if it's something you do with the product (driving a car down a twisted mountain road). They emphasize *being* if there is an ideal fantasy scene that the product is supposed to complete (as do the cigarettes shared by the couple beside a mountain pool). But all the happiness and satisfaction you witness has to stem from or focus on the product. That's what makes the sales pitch effective! Such happiness must be a tangible and superficially observable happiness. After all, you must see and assimilate it in thirty seconds of TV time or five seconds of glancing at a magazine ad. The pride you might feel at a job well done is hard to convey in this format—but not the material reward, such as a trophy or a chocolate chip cookie. Ads go for the deeper feeling of pride or joy, but they focus on the tangible thing about it. After a while, the tangible thing begins to seem the main idea—which it is, from the seller's point of view.

Too narrow a choice. Sure, ads seem to give you the feeling of choice. You, the consumer, can buy whatever you choose. But the one choice you are never given is *whether* to buy or not. The only formula for success or transformation or progress is purchase.

Who Painted This Picture, Anyway?

The first generation of advertisers were often, interestingly enough, sons of ministers (as historian T. J. Jackson Lears has pointed out). These men preached a new faith to America at the beginning of the twentieth century. Victorian Americans were used to saving and producing; ads had to teach modern Americans to spend and consume. Early ads also taught people how to groom themselves and to take care of their health (even if it meant eating a packet of yeast a day, as one company suggested), and that it was normal to be worried or have headaches or hemorrhoids.

A few early critics of advertising saw the practice as a conspiracy. People are legitimately worried about the new order, they said. But instead of letting workers express their frustration with long factory hours and noncreative jobs, those scheming ad-men teach people to further support the new system. The reasoning went something like this: Feel anxious about growing old while working in the factory? Buy this new face cream, a company product, and you'll feel young again. The workers will think they've found satisfaction and renewal; meanwhile, they will be strengthening the company's business by increasing demand for its product. It sounds good in the short run, critics said, but in the long run the frustration will only grow.

Today's generation of advertisers are scientists and psychologists and very precise artists. Building on decades of advertising history and success, they have sophisticated methods of seeing what you want and *suggesting* what you want. The process of selling a product to you begins years before the product hits the shelves and surrounds and suffuses you while you're in the store, pulling you to the shelves almost before you know it. None of this is meant to harm you, of course: companies just want to sell their products. Fears of conspiracy have long since died. Producers are competing with each other, and so are unlikely to share and compare notes—which is illegal, anyway. What's more, American consumers are tough customers who wouldn't buy what they didn't believe they wanted. Indeed, that's why so many new products fail each year.

But sometimes, for some people, sales techniques do cross the line between persuasion and manipulation—especially given modern techniques that operate below your level of consciousness. The next section will introduce you to several you may not know about.

Marketing, the Other Side of the Ad

When a company wants to develop a product, it relies on psychologists, canvassers, artists, business historians—all classed together as marketers—to guide it through every stage of design, advertising, packaging, and display. Generally, these people have studied the science of marketing. Most corporations, even small ones, maintain in-house marketing divisions. Retail stores hire their own marketing experts. Marketing relies on several disciplines, but it is a science with its own textbooks and industry journals. Advanced degrees can be pursued, and there are professors and doctors of marketing. This is the force behind the advertisements you see, hear, and hum. Whether you know it or not, you, as a consumer, are the subject of considerable scholarly attention.

Advertisers may seem to tell you what you want, but they begin by asking what you want. In what ways do you feel unfulfilled? What makes you buy the things you do? What product names and colors and scents bring out the best in you? What emotions, or fears, or desires are the most powerful motivators for you? This isn't idle curiosity: these are questions they ask of "model" consumers throughout the country on a regular basis. The scope of the questioning ranges from obvious product-oriented information (How much would you spend on it?) to personal preferences (What is your favorite holiday? What do you like best about it?) to the most abstract and loony (What type of music does our product listen to?).

The idea behind all of this is not only to sell you a specific product, but to find out what you want to buy. Ideally, of course, you'll reveal a need for a specific product that a company can develop and hand you—such as, say, sweet soda without the sugar. But you might also reveal a deeper need for love and softness, something you'd pay a lot to feel. You might even reveal that you like to have fun and feel pampered on your days off. Whatever your answer, the corporation will make it their business to sell it to you. If it's specifically nonsugary soda you want, and enough other people want it, it will be developed, packaged, and sold. If it's love and softness you want, the company might still market the soda, but sell it by featuring two children playing with a kitten, while the smiling mother looks on, sipping her wholesome no-sugar soda. And if having fun is the only thing they can get from you, they might have a puzzle on the can, or a sweepstakes give-away at the soda display—or feature a group of kids on holiday, sipping the soda and having a ball. Don't laugh: this type of thing works.

Psychographics

How old are you? Where do you live? How much do you earn? Marketers care about your answers to these questions—eliciting such demographic data as age, income, occupation, and education—but not as much as they used to. Today, the basis for defining market segments and identifying potential consumers of a product has evolved into something called *psychographics*. Psychographics refers partly to your lifestyle and partly to your ambitions and hopes and partly to your personal psychology and world-view. It is a technique that allows marketers to focus in specifically on the psychological cues that will make most sense to you as an individual—or, at least, as a specific type. The reasonable assumption is that people don't always identify with their neighbors or their income class or even their families, but that they do follow typical purchasing paths.

General Foods International, for instance, hired a consulting group to market its presweetened instant coffee. It was determined that the target consumers for this coffee were women, but that's not all. Researchers found that likely consumers were college-educated women who had been to Europe or planned to go, who worked but were not zealously ambitious, and who valued both traditional family life and occasional self-indulgence. Women in the study were asked such questions as "How do you feel before you've had a cup of coffee? And after? If you had a dream and General Foods International Coffee played a part, what would it be? How old is GFIC? Is it male or female?" (The study questions were reported by Bernice Kanner in *Working Woman* magazine, 1990.) The women were given drawings of steaming cups of coffee with cartoon dialogue-bubbles to fill in. Such questions let them project their own fantasies and personalities onto the product.

The results were translated into now-familiar packaging and promotion. The product's name always refers to a yummy, self-indulgent, sinful-sounding flavor (hazelnut, chocolate) and to a European country to suggest tradition and sophistication and to pique nostalgia for that college trip: Hazelnut Belgian Coffee, Suisse Mocha Café, and so on. A "special moments" ad campaign features appropriate settings and situations: two friends chat and reminisce about that cute waiter in a Paris café, for instance. Since women in the study turned away from blue light and high-tech images and responded warmly to images of family life and strains of relaxing music, you'll find the latter in the background. Iced coffee was out, since women responded better to warm images than cold. These details may sound trivial, but in high finance the slightest off-image can result in millions of dollars of lost sales.

Anheuser-Busch, to cite a more troublesome example, determined that its target population of beer drinkers were blue-collar males who felt underappreciated in their work and in their lives. Their solution was a campaign built around the slogan "This Bud's for all you do." Schlitz beer targeted a similar population of macho men who worked hard and believed they had too little time for pleasure. They offered the campaign "You only go around once, so you might as well reach for all the gusto you can!" Both ad campaigns picked up on deep feelings and redirected them towards the company product, beer.

The shift to psychographics is an important development in marketing science. It may be argued that this approach is a way of giving consumers more of exactly what they want. Indeed, GFIC discovered that women wanted sugar-free coffees in 1984 and decaf versions in 1989 and they developed both—surely no harm in that. But it may also be said that in its minutely specific targeting, ads today hold greater potential for manipulative and exploitative results.

When Ads Push Your Buttons

Of course no one is brainwashing anyone, particularly shrewd American consumers who relish their luxury of choice. But ads have become psychologically sophisticated and can push your buttons without your even knowing why they hit so deep. Marketers tailor their messages to fit the goal of improving business. This goal is not the same as the aim of your psychological well-being—even though that may seem to be what the ad promises.

In the GFIC commercial, women respond to the warmth in the commercial, not the specific information about processed coffee beans. (And respond they do: between 1989 and 1990, while these ads ran, General Foods sold $115.9 million worth of their International Coffees, 11 percent higher than in the same period the previous year. Meanwhile, sales of regular instant coffee decreased by 9.1 percent.) It's become commonplace, but it is interesting to note how little product information is conveyed in the typical commercial or advertisement. The most effective ads sell feelings. But such ads raise needs and desires and promise feelings that the product itself can't possibly fill. Perhaps women who drink GFIC will feel some fleeting warmth, but the commercial leaves them with piqued and unresolved nostalgia, a longing for family love, and a deepening sense of the need for self-indulgence. It validates their sense that they need warmth and love and reward—and makes it look as if others have it and they don't. The "solution": the company's coffee.

Beer commercials are just as frustrating. The commercials validate the viewers' sense of feeling underappreciated or unrewarded for all they do. By this gesture, the commercial and the company win the viewers' sympathy. But that sympathy and acknowledgment of need are redirected toward the company's product. It offers the false promise that drinking beer will resolve that feeling of underappreciation. When that doesn't work, as of course it won't, the consumer will probably purchase still more beer in an effort to reach satisfaction. And so the false path to happiness is paved.

Taking Control

Marketers are not responsible for the well-being of society or for your psychological satisfaction. They want to sell a product. In the course of meeting their business aims, however, many happen to unearth real problems and desires. They offer as solution a single product—which can't, of course, solve the problem. In the absence of a mass conscience in them about raising and abandoning such needs, you, the consumer, need to be aware and to take control.

Once ads tap a deep psychological level, it becomes difficult to remain rational about them. You respond without knowing just what you're responding to. And your response can be a powerful, gut-level reaction. To the extent that you stop being in control of your response to a pitch for a material product, you are being exploited. The means of the exploitation are deep needs that exist within you; these needs are used to fill someone else's aim. Not that this is a malevolent enterprise meant to doom you. It just means that you have to keep your own needs and goals in clear view.

Chapter 9, "Fighting Back," offers several ideas for responding to the strong pull of this type of advertising. You will see that the trick involves understanding your own desires clearly and understanding the advertiser's message clearly. Simply paying attention can help you remain rational about ads. From that point, a dose of solid logic and personal insight can turn TV-watching from a threat into a game.

Experiential Shopping

The psychological approach takes it for granted that shoppers will head out when they need a certain product or feeling or whatever. But is this the only thing leading shoppers to the store? How do consumers really make their decisions? Most college economics classes teach that consumers are rational, thinking animals who process various kinds of incoming information and make logical decisions based on value and availability. These decisions can even be charted on "preference curves," numerical values assigned to relative pleasure and dissatisfaction with products and services. For years, marketers worked along these lines. They pitched their goods by relying on an appeal to value or style or rationality. Recently, however, a new model for the consumer has been developed: a model that sees the common consumer as a fun-seeker who values the entertainment aspect of shopping. This shift to an "experiential" view of consumption is another major recent shift in marketing.

According to the experiential view, shoppers head out in search of a variety of sensory experiences, not just the products they will ultimately buy. As a shopper, you know what they mean: that dazzling array of colors, products, other shoppers, holiday decorations, music, food, *life*, that makes you feel anything (from worldly success to migraine headache) is possible. The experiential view holds that this feeling may be just what you seek, and not necessarily the product itself. In fact, as a compulsive shopper, the wisdom is that you are particularly motivated by the experiential aspect of shopping.

Just as advertisements have found ways to tap into your deep desires for youth, beauty, belonging, excelling, and so on, marketers of the experiential school are now exploring ways to tap into your need for activity, social interaction, symbolic meaning, emotional stimulation, even fantasy. The hope, of course, is that all of these desires and needs can be redirected into shopping—can be used to lure you into stores, provided by the experience of shopping, and rewarded at the moment of purchase. No matter how noble or instinctive or nonmaterialistic your aims, someone is trying to direct those aims back into materialism.

Evidence points to the fact that shoppers with experiential, entertainment goals are particularly susceptible to nonrational cues: things you hear, smell, feel in the background. This makes sense when you consider that the left side of your brain, the less rational, more creative side, is involved in experience and entertainment. (The right side is involved in rational decisions; it answers to an old-fashioned appeal to value and need.) Today's marketers are toying with smells, sounds, visual arrangements, and other nonrational cues to lure you into a store in a swoon of sentimentality, an onslaught of starvation...whatever will motivate you powerfully, even if you don't know where these feelings come from.

Music. Music has long been known to reach deep within people's minds, memories, and souls. In a simple way, this knowledge has been translated into advertising jingles that stick with you for life. But today's marketers want to go beyond that. Is there some type of music that will stimulate shopping among a certain target group? Can particular music be used to trigger particular emotions and desires? Marketers are willing to bet that it can and have gone to some lengths to find out just how it works. As one researcher named Gordon C. Bruner II noted, striking a chilling chord, appropriately structured music acts on the nervous system like a key on a lock, activating brain processes with corresponding emotional reactions.

In one study, researchers recorded the emotional expressions of subjects upon hearing various tones and beats and textures of music. They found, for instance, that music with two beats per measure produced "a rigid and controlled expression in comparison with triple rhythm, which is more relaxed or abandoned." And "the timbre of brass instruments conveys a feeling of cold, hard force whereas reed instruments produce a lonely, melancholy expression." And "complex harmonies are more agitated and sad than simple harmonies, which are more serene and happy." Does that mean that happy music will play in stores? Another study cited by Bruner suggests the opposite: "Happy music produced happier moods in subjects, but sad music produced the highest purchase intentions." How interesting: it sounds as if shoppers might be brought by sad music to brood on their lives and situations—ever so much gloomier than the glitter around them in stores—and end up purchasing costly items to make themselves feel better.

Customers in one restaurant who listened to slow music took more time to eat their meals than customers in the same restaurant on another night who listened to fast music; the result, a greater wait for tables and a higher sales volume at the bar. The researcher who conducted this study also tested fast and slow music in a supermarket, and discovered that the slower music led shoppers to spend more time shopping, thus filling their baskets higher and bringing sales volume up. Loud music seems to bring greater sales volume per minute than soft music, even though shoppers spend less overall time in the store—perhaps they rush in and out, to escape the cacophony! And music seems most powerful when shoppers are buying items involving little rational thought but high emotional/symbolic/aesthetic value, such as jewelry, sportswear, cosmetics, and beer. (You'll hear less music around cars, computers, cameras, and insurance.) If it all sounds very specific, researchers still express frustration that the science of music manipulation has not progressed further. "Music has been treated too generally in most past marketing studies," writes Bruner, "with interest merely in its presence or absence in some treatment. Significant new knowledge will not be acquired until individual components of music are manipulated, examined, and/or controlled."

One drug chain with almost 2000 stores hired two companies to create a customized, in-house radio-like program, with special ads and music. The companies targeted impulse buyers in particular. After all, research revealed that decisions for two of every three purchases were made in the store. Candy and gum, cosmetics, and oral hygiene were the most susceptible to impulse purchasing, so a drug store seemed a good place to try it out. The result? An average 20 percent increase in sales. One women's clothing store chain that prides itself on an international ambience pipes in prerecorded, custom-tailored French music and commentary. Just being in the store can make you feel foreign, young, sophisticated, and happy.

You've seen the music videos in juniors' clothing departments: obviously, these stores are targeting teens. The familiar music lures them in, and the videos keep them transfixed to the screen—where they see the latest styles sported by singers positively bursting with self-confidence, sex appeal, and success. When they look back down to reality: presto! Similar items on racks promise their own magic. But that's not the only reason the music videos are there. Time speeds up when you listen to music you know and like: an hour passes when you might have sworn it was ten minutes. The result: you stay in the store for the time it takes to break down your resistance to buying whatever's on display. Live pianists are brought into "classy" department stores for the same reasons. The place seems classier; you linger because you want to be the kind of person who enjoys this type of music (and can afford to shop in these designer departments). You'll also feel valued and respected as a shopper; after all, someone is going to considerable lengths to entertain you. That all ties into the fantasy aspect of shopping: you can play someone you're not, in a class beyond your own. You can even pretend you're out at a cultural event and buy a more elegant dress for the occasion.

Aroma. Your ears aren't the only sense organ that can expect assault. Imagine the warm, hearty, homey smell of bread baking. Wouldn't you follow it where it led, especially if it led straight to a bakery counter? Think of a bowl of potpourri, some spiced-apple and cinnamon scent that reminded you of autumn with your grandmother. Wouldn't you linger over silk scarves a bit longer, if a bowl of the stuff were right there? Marketers, too, smell business.

No sense is more closely connected to memory than scent. Even if you can't identify a particular smell, it can elicit images and associations from deep within your experience. A whiff can transport you back over years and miles and trigger the same emotions you felt when you first encountered it. Some scents have the same effect on everyone. Peppermint, lemon, rosemary, eucalyptus, and pine seem to make most people come alive, wake up, feel vibrant and alert. Lavender, clove, flowers, and woodlands have an opposite effect, calming and soothing jangled nerves. And what could be more pleasant or uplifting than walking into an area suffused in a cheery citrus mixture—especially if you've been shopping all day? A citrus scent is generally classed as refreshing.

Aroma research is a happening field in marketing these days. The right smell can make shoppers linger or relax or step into fantasy. One saleswoman routinely burns a specific brand of scented candles she discovered, because she says she sees her customers relax and enjoy shopping more, as Molly O'Neill reported in a 1991 *New York Times* article. Others use potpourri, sprays, even turntable-like aroma "stereos" or central-air-conditioning ducts to diffuse aromas. Companies such as Aromasys in Richfield, Minnesota, receive requests from universities and corporations to develop specific mood-altering fragrance systems. At the headquarters of Shimuzu, a Tokyo-based corporation, clients are seated in a reception area where the floor is scented with a subtle woodsy aroma. "It's like an aromatic Quaalude," an executive told O'Neill.

Architecture. From the arrangement of items in each store to the construction of the building itself, shopping space is designed to lure you in and keep you there. This is true from the corner boutique to the neighborhood department store—and most especially in that modern mecca of consumption, the mall.

Someone, somewhere, decided that consumers begin to spend serious money in their third hour of shopping. Perhaps defenses are lowest then, or perhaps shoppers become frustrated at their empty-handedness despite a morning's (evening's, afternoon's) activity. Maybe shoppers simply become convinced that they've made their comparisons and are ready to invest in the best. For whatever reason, and whether the assumption is true or not, just about everything in a shopping mall is designed to keep you there for at least three hours. They're doing something right. In 1986, consumers spent 1 trillion dollars, 54 percent of it in shopping centers, as Carolyn Wesson noted in *Women Who Shop Too Much*.

Think about getting to the mall in the first place. Before you even leave home, chances are you've allotted several hours for the adventure. Malls are typically distant from urban centers: to get there, you have to drive some distance, park, and walk across that sea of chrome and pavement to the entrance. You must, of course, have a car in the first place—if you can't afford a car, you probably couldn't afford to buy much in the mall, and so you're not wanted. But even with a car, the trip involves an investment of time: it's unlikely you'd buy a carton of milk and dash back out and drive home. Just in case you would, though, you'll almost never find a supermarket as part of a large indoor mall. Perishables might not wait three hours to be driven home...but they're hoping that you will.

Once you're inside, try looking around for the time of day— chances are you won't find a single indicator. It is rare to find a clock in a mall; the centerpiece is more likely to be a fountain or a sculpture or a café. The pretty center atrium is unlikely to have real windows through which you could see outside and contrast the reality of trees and sky to the artificial environment. The changing daylight would remind shoppers that time was passing. (An occasional skylight may illuminate the mall's tree display and make it seem a natural oasis.) A shopping mall is its own unique environment, with its own climate and season and air- and traffic-flow. Outside changes of light and season and weather that might lead you to feel tired or ready for change are replaced in the mall by a man-made, controlled environment, one that keeps you as alert and as ready to buy as possible.

The layout of the mall is designed to route you past the maximum number of stores. If you've ever looked for a specific item, such as shoes, you'll note that you can't just go to one shoe store after another, all in a row. Far from it. Even if the mall has thirty different shoe stores, they will be spread out carefully throughout every floor and section of the mall. Just as escalators and stairs tend to lead you past stores and goods instead of straight up, your search for shoes will lead you on a treasure hunt through every inch of the mall. And if you go shopping with a member of the opposite sex, you'll note that you two do better sticking together. No male's section in one area, female's in another: that might encourage you to split up, save time, and each miss half the mall. Shoe stores for women will alternate with stereo stores for men, which will alternate with shoe stores for men and lingerie shops for both of you. And that's not even counting restaurants, video games, beauty salons, and swimming pools with dolphins.

That's right, dolphins. One shopping mall deep in Canada, where the winters are severe and the people apparently hungry for distraction, boasts the world's largest retail/entertainment space, including such goodies as the world's seventh largest *fleet of underwater submarines*. The West Edmonton Mall covers 5.2 million square feet, or 115 American football fields. In addition to its 800-odd stores, 19 movie theaters, and 110 eating establishments, the mall houses the world's largest indoor amusement park, an NHL-size ice skating rink, miniature golf, a water park, a lagoon—that's where the dolphins and the subs come in—and a hotel. It's an extreme case of retail extravaganza, but it points to a serious marketing concept.

People would leave a mall if they felt hungry. They might certainly leave if they felt tired or grungy or bored. But if all these needs are filled *right there*, why go anywhere else? That's one reason malls are such complete entertainment—and beauty, and athletic, and social interaction—centers. Of course, these businesses also want to be there because they benefit from the built-in traffic flow in the mall. Every store has the potential to attract customers who come specifically for another store. Everyone in the selling game wins.

Malls can be great fun. They provide a common space for social interaction, much as the old-fashioned marketplace did. They certainly provide visual distraction, in people-watching, store displays, and the overall attractiveness of the place. A mall might even seem the fantasy city, with no litter on the streets, no beggars, perfect weather and lush foliage, and helpful workers (salespeople) everywhere you go. The illusion is that it's public space for everyone—although it's not, of course. If you ever want to remind yourself that a mall is private space carefully controlled by management, try passing out leaflets for an individual organization or cause. Try taking pictures—which most mall owners won't allow without permission. You'll be reminded that you are welcome as a customer and a "stroller," but no more. All the fun you experience in the mall is an appeal to the experiential side of shopping.

Wares everywhere you go. You don't have to go all the way to the mall to enjoy fancy display marketing. Within most stores, including those in the mall, goods are arranged to lure you in. Sale items are in the back, routing you past items with the highest markup. Each aisle is designed for maximum exposure of merchandise, and together the aisles are designed to direct you past the largest proportion of selling area. Your local supermarket uses the same tricks. Most supermarkets survive by offering goods at a very limited markup: just a penny or two per item. This makes it essential that they sell goods at a significant rate. Of course, there are some higher markup items, and these are all placed at eye-level. Bargain brands are usually on the highest and lowest shelves—unless it's a brand made by the store you're in. The hope is that in your rush and supposed efficiency, you'll grab what you see first and pay more.

The assumption behind in-store marketing—or merchandising, as its known—is that most consumer decisions are made at "point of purchase." According to the self-serving figures of the Point-of-Purchase Advertising Institute (POPAI), decisions for two of every three purchases are made in the store. That accounts for the candy and gum and fancy bottles, boxes, and magazines at the supermarket checkout. It also accounts for the emphasis on packaging and in-store display.

The fancier techniques go after impulse shoppers. One large deli in a big city offers credit card shopping, as do more and more supermarkets. With Visa and MasterCard capabilities, shoppers have unlimited buying potential; and so the deli has begun to stock more expensive items, including nonfood items. Impulse buyers are the target. And, indeed, the resulting increase in sales has so far more than made up for the cost of the credit card processing.

Most supermarkets feature their main attraction at the entrance: fancy baked goods, for instance, or lavish produce. These high-selling, colorful items lure you in and get you in the mood to fill your basket high. From there, a store usually routes you around the entire perimeter in your quest for the basic necessities: milk, butter, eggs, juice. One supermarket in California is experimenting with a "power alley" of produce, meats, fish, and deli products in the center of the store. They put other common grocery items around the perimeter, such as paper products, health and beauty aids, and highly promoted specials. "A more open structure gives customers added latitude in utilizing their shopping time," explained a store executive in a 1988 *Ad Age* story. "The physical layout is expected to enhance impulse buying." However supermarkets choose to do it, you'll end up touring more of the store than you'd imagine. For some people, this is a plus—they stumble across items they needed all along. For others, it's a hassle. Of course, there's a solution for shoppers who don't even like stores very much.

Shopping at home. What an inspiration! Pieces of glamor and glitter and comfort sailing into your mailbox on a regular basis for you to savor, mull over, try on, even purchase, without ever leaving your armchair. For those of limited patience or time, catalog shopping is a boon, offering all the thrills of a real store with few of the headaches and hassles. There's never a wait to park, never someone in line ahead of you, and no dizzying overstimulation of the feet, ears, and eyes. What you choose to focus on is your business.

Of course, it's the business of the catalog designer as well. More so than in stores, you see all the fashions modeled by lithe young beauties—and who wouldn't picture a touch of that youth and beauty rubbing off onto them with the purchase of the same clothing? Catalogs allow retailers complete control of environment: a woodsy setting for outdoor gear, with happy ruddy-cheeked models; a tropical sunset for spandex bikinis, with happy bronze-bodied models. Fantasies become vivid in catalogs, just as they do in all storybooks and in the mall. You place yourself right into the picture.

But the fun doesn't end there. As soon as you pick up the phone to place an order—as you can 24 hours a day, toll-free in many catalogs—you've got a friend and a voice of support on the opposite end of the phone. It's so easy! Just a few numbers, a description of color or size, and that fantasy package is on its way to you. And after you've described your item, the well-mannered, well-trained sales rep on the other end (whose name you'll probably know by now) will ask for the number of your next item. There's nothing judgmental in his or her voice; it could be 3:00 a.m., you could be calling across the country for a flannel bathrobe you'll never need in your sunny state, and it only seems to make the salesperson happy. In fact, that leading question about your next item seems a setup for disappointment if you don't come up with something fast. For the insomniac brooding about life's deprivations, the friendly voice on the phone is hard to give up. So, you think, maybe just a few more items. After all, he or she seems to expect it. And with just a few words from you, comfort is dropped into the mail addressed to you. Add to that the seeming promise of a cashless purchase, and the fantasy is complete.

This scenario is a bit extreme, perhaps, but that feeling of friendship and respect can be a powerful appeal to many shoppers. That's why all the finer stores greet you when you walk in. They know that treating you with respect is the key to making you act with respect toward them and their business—by purchasing and praising the experience to your friends. That's also why the shopping channel holds such powerful appeal to its many addicted viewers. The announcers are all so friendly, so interested in each other's lives, so interested in the stories of viewers who call in. They simulate deep friendship with each other, dropping in on another announcer's program to visit, just as good neighbors and women friends might do. And they invite you to join them—not just as friends who welcome your input, but as friends who share your appreciation of material niceties.

The shopping channel combines the appeal of two addictive, all-consuming pursuits: shopping and television. Each offers enough sensory stimulation to create a complete world around you—perhaps a world you find prettier, friendlier, more alive than your real world. It's as easy to "fall into" television as it is into stores, to lose all sense of time and become mesmerized by the parade of faces and ideas and colors. You might even feel you're more in touch with the world, meeting people and participating in an endless flow of communication and information. After all, aren't people arriving at the store from all over town, or calling in to the channel from all over the country, to connect and share? (Don't you look to see what other people are wearing? Don't you listen to callers describing their nieces' tastes?) And when they do so they operate according to "objective" information in the form of styles and prices and rules of conduct and etiquette. It's a society of shoppers.

Watching the shopping channel makes it all seem "normal." Listen to all those people, calling in to buy so many things! Hear all the respect and encouragement they receive from the announcers! Twenty-four hours a day this goes on, people calling in, buying things, comparing values, and describing material satisfaction in common terms of want and need.

The thing to remember is that shopping may be common, and it may be popular, but it is only "normal" in a relative sense. "What were taken to be normal spending patterns in America in the 1980s...probably hadn't seemed normal since Germany in the days of the Weimar Republic," writes cultural critic Lawrence Shames. "In most other times and places, people went into hock in the face of catastrophe, not each time they wanted a new pair of boots." Shames was writing about money, describing America's "virtually universal consumer indebtedness," but he points to the problem of attitude as well. What happens when shopping becomes the central activity, in terms of time and identity and concern, in people's lives? Like any addiction, it takes over, warping perspective on what's really "normal," or healthy.

Mary: A Warning Story

On the evening of October 20, 1991, a woman named Mary placed a call to one of the TV shopping channels. In some ways it was an ordinary call, and in some ways it was extraordinary.

Mary's house had just been ordered evacuated because of a fire, raging just blocks away and creeping towards her house. Her car was packed and in her driveway. Neighbors were fleeing for their lives; the sky was black with smoke. Mary had changed TV channels away from emergency broadcast news to the shopping channel, which was featuring a ring with a pear-shaped, simulated gemstone. She called in to say she had a similar item.

"I love it and I wear it with a lot of my Spanish clothes that I got from south of the border," Mary told both pitchwoman and national audience. "I get more compliments on it." For a little while they chatted up the ring.

By the way, Mary added, she couldn't linger on the phone. "I have to take off because we're being evacuated. This is a disaster area and I've got the trunk of my car packed with all my pictures and all my [jewelry]."

The amazed saleswoman asked Mary where she was calling from. Mary answered "Berkeley, California, there's a big fire here," and then went on with the conversation. "I love this ring and everybody compliments me on it."

"It's important that you get out of town," the pitchwoman advised. "We'll worry about your [ring] tomorrow. OK?" Mary hung up, presumably to drive away.

The ring may not have been foremost on Mary's mind. Perhaps she needed human contact with someone "normal," someone who wasn't packing a life into the trunk of a car while watching neighbors flee. Perhaps she craved the familiar ritual of calling in to talk about some nice object—shopping was the calming drug she used to defuse her anxiety. She may just have needed reassurance that material goods couldn't ever be all lost, there would always be "more where that came from." But Mary from Berkeley had her priorities confused, to say the least. Shopping was symptomatic of her loss of perspective; at the moment of evacuation, it was all she could think of, when her very life was in danger. Mary might have done well to examine these issues—before it reached crisis point.

Fantasies and the Compulsive Shopper

Compulsive shoppers seem to have a higher capacity for fantasy than average shoppers. This is what allows them to escape negative feelings by shopping or to imagine that the world they're bringing home is the world afforded them by their credit cards, if not their bank balance. Looking at store displays and slender mannequins, compulsive shoppers may be particularly able to project themselves into the tableau of success and social triumph. And with music swelling in the background, familiar childhood smells wafting through the air, and sales staff catering with deference to the shopper, the fantasy goes on.

With the shift to psychographics and experiential shopping, compulsive shoppers are increasingly the target of sales pitches. Psychographics tap the fantasies, and appeals to experiential shopping feed them. It can be hard to remain rational in the face of such calls—especially when your shopping behavior doesn't seem rational to yourself! But remaining rational is the first step towards recovery.

The point to all of this is to remain aware. That strong urge you often feel to go shopping or to keep shopping may not come entirely from you—more likely it comes partly from you (as a need for some feeling), only to be fanned and encouraged by people whose business it is to understand you and to keep you shopping. This may be in their best interest, but it's not always in yours. Begin paying attention to the urges that pull you into stores. Focus in on rational need first—and if that doesn't work, focus on your senses one at a time. Is there a smell you're following to the bakery section? Is there music that brings back sad feelings from your childhood, making you want to console yourself with a purchase? Is there music that makes you feel happy and proud (and worthy of a fancy dress) or that makes you feel like dancing, reviving you when you've already spent many hours shopping? Perhaps there's even something indefinable that catches your eye, pretty colors or a bold "Sale!" sign. These can work nonrationally, too. Merely becoming conscious of such factors can help you recognize them for what they are—whether simple sensory stimulations or deep underlying needs—and satisfy them in some way not directly threatening to your bank balance! (More about this in chapter 9, "Fighting Back.")

Taking Care of Yourself

Think for a moment about what it means to be a "consumer." A consumer is someone who *uses*, instead of produces. A good consumer is someone who uses up, in fact, so that he or she needs more. Just think of that word "consumption"; it once referred to a wasting disease. *Consume* is what fires do as they eat up houses and neighborhoods, anything in their destructive path. Today it still means taking in, ingesting, making an external thing a part of yourself. Isn't there more you want to do with your time and your energy? Wouldn't you rather define yourself by what you do or who you are than by what you have and wear and use?

But wait, you say. The experiential view of shopping suggests an objective very different from materialism. After all, the activity of shopping is something you do, not something you have. If you head out to the mall in search of fun and fantasy or social interaction and exercise, you are shopping for much more than the concrete purchase. Indeed, problem shoppers might just as easily substitute other stimulating activities for shopping—say reading or dancing—activities that won't lead to material purchase. But the problem is, for most people in this society who value the fun and activity of shopping, material goods still *seem* the reward and the goal. You may feel that you haven't really shopped correctly or successfully unless you have something to show for it: a trophy for the race. The various calls to shop teach you to think of the material purchase as the main idea, not the experience of shopping. You may go out for fun, but you still come back in debt.

And where do compulsive shoppers fit into this scheme of things? Do they have a higher desire for material goods than "normal" shoppers, or a higher desire for external stimulation in the form of shopping? One option favors the rational view of shopping, the other the experiential. The answer, of course, is that neither serves as an answer for everyone. Probably, most compulsive shoppers feel some blend of the two, and some one more than the other. Research into other compulsive behaviors, such as drinking, eating, and gambling, suggests that compulsive shoppers might indulge in their behavior to escape painful feelings in a blur of fantasy—the experience of shopping is what matters. But help might also come from the consolation of external things, as if each new object brought an infusion of strength and meaning into the person's seemingly empty life—in other words, material goods do matter. One thing's for sure: marketers will continue to try reaching everyone, using every approach possible. And the behavior of compulsive shoppers will be fanned and encouraged, whatever their motivations.

In thinking about your shopping habits, it might help to think about which of these motivations—experience or materialism—enforces your own shopping behavior. How materialistic are you, really? Remember, materialism in itself is not necessarily a positive or a negative trait—but the extremes can be dangerous. You can see how too much materialism can lead to greed and eternal dissatisfaction; but too little can become its own mania, leading to deprivation, asceticism, even anorexia, as Russell Belk notes. If you find you're not terribly attached to objects, perhaps there is something in the experience of shopping that motivates you. Just what is it about shopping that makes you feel better? You won't find an answer right away. But in the course of this book, it's a question that should be foremost in your mind. An answer will allow you to substitute new activities, outlooks, and solutions for your old destructive behaviors and to meet your needs in a heathier way. Self-awareness is the place to begin.

4

Discovering Why
You Shop

For instance, I set out to run errands one day with
the intent to tie up loose ends before I got down
to the business of working on a design project.
What should I happen to run across? A massive
sidewalk sale, what else. I heard the little voice in
my head say "Get away, don't walk closer," but
the voice became a whimper as I heard the roar of
the crowd and smelled the smell of a good deal.
The frantic search for a bargain was in the air as
people darted about—even in 95 degree heat, drip-
ping sweat, drooling. I allowed myself to be pulled
into the fervor and bought almost the first thing
that appealed—an incomplete set of china. My rationale? I had one piece of this set at home that I
paid three times as much for. WHAT A DEAL. I

had to have it. Next came bins of mismatched
frames and loads of 75 percent-off matted posters
and prints that I *knew* would make perfect little
gifts in years to come. WHAT A DEAL. I had to
have them. In less than an hour, I had spent $100,
all under the guise of saving money when I really
needed these things in the future. But what about
my insurance payment due now? I began to giggle
hysterically as I returned to pick up my bag of
china—the salespersons looked at me curiously.
"Would you believe it if I told you I'm using shopping to avoid something?" I said. Their curious
stares turned blank. I turned to go, beginning to
allow myself to explore what compelled me here.
What was I avoiding? By now I'm good enough at
this to be less afraid of my anxieties—and to level
with myself. "Okay, self," I said, "there's something you don't want to face up to, isn't there?"
"Of course," I answered, "I don't want to begin
that project I told myself I'd start today."
—*Confessions of Jane, a self-professed shopping addict.*

At the moment of purchase, everyone has a rationale for why
they must buy what they buy. WHAT A DEAL is the theme of the
day for Jane—she convinces herself that the bargain is just too good
to pass up. She can't imagine not having it. She gives in to her
impulse. It feels good to be so smart to find such a buy, never
mind the pending bills lying at home on the dining room table.
The immediacy of the moment overrides objectivity.

Her actions have a desperateness, as if, if she lets this bargain
go, she will never find another. Fortunately she has some control
over her habit when she catches herself in the act. She quickly real-
izes that she is not only falling back on typical impulsive behavior,
but also avoiding something. The anxiety of her project is so
powerful that she unconsciously sets out to delay the anxiety as
long as she can with frantic shopping behavior. Not only that, the
"positive" stress she feels from mingling in the sweaty crowd and
being the first to pounce on a bargain may distract her from the

"negative" stress she feels about getting started on a difficult task. This is classic avoidance behavior—confuse the issue with as many competing stresses as possible!

Add to these the stress of explaining her "bargains" to her husband (that is, if she chooses to reveal her purchases). Hopefully they'll have a long and hearty discussion late into the night, and she won't have to start her project at all.

The above scenario illustrates just a few of the "shopping drives" that propel people to shop compulsively. There are many reasons why people choose to spend their time and money this way—the permutations of compulsive shopping behavior are endless. For this reason, the vast amount of information pertaining to compulsive behavior and shopping in particular has been grouped into eight of the most commonly experienced impulses. Keep in mind that these are organized in such a way as to clarify and help you avoid feeling overwhelmed at first with all the reasons you shop.

The eight common impulses are:

1. You shop to elevate your sense of self-worth.

2. You shop as a diversionary tactic.

3. You shop to vent hostility, or conversely, to demonstrate love.

4. You shop to fill a void of loneliness.

5. You shop to compensate feelings of deprivation.

6. You shop for immediate gratification.

7. You shop to relieve depression.

8. You shop due to a perceived loss of control.

You may instantly discover yourself in one description, or you may recognize yourself in a combination of two or more. Sift through them and hunt for your bargain.

Since at first most people tend to feel overwhelmed with the problem of compulsive shopping, remember that at this point you are in the stage of discovery, not judgment. If you catch yourself making belittling remarks while you read, saying such things as "How awful," "What a creep I am," or "How can a person be so stupid?" you will only block yourself. You will be closing yourself off to the possibility of getting beyond your self-deprecating statements to look at what contributes to them. Allow yourself to read without self-condemnation, to absorb the material. Later on you can choose to accept what is true for you and what you may choose to act on.

If you sense that your spending behavior is unconscious—that is, that you are not aware of underlying motives you may harbor—then you will want to spend some time getting closer to those motives. Where do they come from? What triggers them? How will you know when your shopping behavior is a mask for something else going on (or not going on) in your life?

Eight Common Impulses That Drive Compulsive Shoppers

1. You shop to elevate your sense of self-worth. For better or worse, a key problem of compulsive shoppers is low self-esteem. Surrounded by pristine mall glitziness, you imagine you are someone else. You escape your "humdrum" existence to the world of perfect mannequins, unwrinkled clothes, multiple choices. The choices are exciting, dazzling. All those choices and colors make you feel good, help you forget that you are a real person with problems, a house to clean and bills to pay. You're just not good enough as you are. If you are someone struggling to make ends meet and dream of being wealthy someday, the illusion of being a rich person in a store full of rich peoples' delights is powerful. For a moment you can forget and pretend. Hours in the immaculate mall climate spell relief—until you leave.

You perceive that the act of purchasing increases your sense of self-worth and esteem. You shrug off your inability to afford something or to pay cash. You spend time window-shopping to remind yourself of what "could be" rather than what is. And window-shopping can be a dangerous activity for those bent on spending—it sets you up for an opportunity to buy.

2. You shop as a diversionary tactic. Perhaps you experience shopping as an absolute must. The drive to go shopping and buy something is so all-consuming that it overpowers the little voice reminding you of something you need to take care of. Maybe you are avoiding something you don't want to do. Or avoiding someone you don't want to see. You perceive that the act of shopping becomes equally important or even more important than the thing you are avoiding.

The key word here is "perceive." You are engaging in a mind game of "I think I'll ignore something and hope it goes away." You give in to your desire to avoid, and so tell yourself that the thing you must buy is very, very important. Hence the perception that shopping itself is very important.

One compulsive shopper said that whenever she felt put down by her spouse, she would simultaneously experience an urge to purchase some specific thing (for example, the perfect set of hair curlers). Perhaps the drive would be triggered by seeing a catalog lying on the table. She would pick up the catalog and begin obsessing, thereby replacing the anxiety that belonged to the marriage. "This set has eight curlers, has wet heat, is five dollars more than this set which has only six—but let's see, I'm planning to get my hair cut next month, so that may be the ideal one to buy, and then I would save five dollars..." and so on. She has now effectively put off dealing with her husband for the length of time she spent ruminating over the catalog. Her marriage problems won't go away, and so her anxiety is only temporarily "cured" by the curlers. She will feel anxious and shop again and again until she *recognizes* that she is anxious, and that her anxiety drives her behavior.

3a. You shop to vent hostility. Consciously or unconsciously you know that someone will be upset with you if you rampantly spend. You may want that person to notice you. Perhaps you're not sure how to ask for what you want or need, and so you go about it indirectly. You spend until they pay attention. Although it's not as direct as a punch or a slap, this type of behavior is still aggressive. Unfortunately, it's too indirect to be helpful, and it usually ends up hurting *you*. The key question is where does the hostility come from? To ask this question, you will need to begin searching inside yourself. Anger is usually a sign that something is buried, and if you take time to uncover and confront the basis for your anger, you will benefit in the long run.

On the other hand, let's say you damn well *know* that you're angry and that you purchase items you don't need to "get back" at someone rather than deal directly with your feelings. These conscious motives are at another level—and that's good, because they are on the surface and can be recognized. But now you need to deal with them constructively, to channel them into more creative pursuits that produce results other than depleting your bank account.

3b. Conversely, you shop to demonstrate love. Some shoppers feel extremely insecure, fearing that others do not love them enough or disapprove of them or may leave them. They feel the need to produce constant tangible proof of their worthiness through gifts. For example, one woman had difficulty most of her long life expressing love to her children and grandchildren. She would become very uncomfortable and remove herself from the situation if any kind of verbal or physical communication threatened to become too intimate. Instead, she would devise excuses for unexpected, spontaneous gifts. While her gift-giving could be interpreted harmlessly as generous proof of love, such behavior becomes useless and nonfunctional if overdone to the point of jeopardizing one's financial health. This indirect form of self-expression may be a cultural throwback to other times, when proof of a mother's love was in food, material care, and gifts. With the impact of the women's liberation movement in the sixties and seventies, a gradual shift has occurred where women, as well as men, can express themselves more directly through words and actions, rather than indirectly through gifts.

4. You shop to fill a void of loneliness. Maybe you are experiencing a sense of loss right now, and you feel bored, anxious, painfully alone. You arrange your schedule so that you can be at the mall on nights and weekends to create the feeling of connectedness with other people and places. The store is a familiar place, a known quantity. Rather than muster the bravery you think it requires to risk meeting new people, you spend time going through the motions of being with people by rubbing shoulders with strangers. This creates the illusion of community, but the community is only an image.

One man, recently widowed, found himself wandering through the stores daily, just to fill time and avoid going home. Shopping helps the grieving person feel distracted, so that he or she can put off dealing with loss. Granted, some amount of distraction can be a solace to the grieving person—shopping or another activity can provide a bit of relief which can act as a much needed "break" from turmoil. But when you indulge in too much shopping, you are acting in a compulsive way to avoid something else. You may be searching for something that simply can't be found in a store.

5. You shop to compensate for feelings of deprivation. Perhaps you anticipate future hardships, and act as if binging before a diet or smoking too many cigarettes before you quit. Or maybe you remember past hard times and you want to make up for losses. Some people who endured the Depression found themselves overspending in later years whether they could afford it or not. One woman reported that she was inexplicably drawn to purchasing dresses whenever she could, so that she had closets and closets full of unworn dresses with the tags still on them. When she took the time to examine her behavior and gain some insight, she understood that she was compensating for the poverty she had experienced in her adolescent years, when she only had one dress.

6. You shop for immediate gratification. Times are still tough, and today's world of failing banks and recession gives many people the feeling that they won't ever get beyond their present socioeconomic circumstances and into a life of comparative abundance. Maybe buying something now will be the salve for that "wound." You work hard and put up with a lot of dirt, and so you deserve it, right? Despite your long-term financial goals or ambitions, you fall prey to the need to gratify your shopping whims immediately. You feel hopeless at ever being able to get ahead, and so you spend in the short run rather than save for the long run.

Or you easily succumb to the comments of friends and family when they say, "Honey, you work so hard—and you earn your own money, don't you? Go ahead!" These well-meaning folks don't realize that they're acting as enablers to the shopper's addiction. They're just echoing society's values.

Perhaps you've never fancied yourself a self-controlled saver. You think you lack the discipline to go without until you can afford something. You allow the "I can have it all" generation's rampant consumerism to rub off on you. And you especially enjoy the "high" or adrenaline rush of the purchase, much like a quick drug fix providing instant release, masking the long-term costs.

7. You shop to relieve depression. The act of purchasing diverts you from feeling depressed. Your feelings are at an all-time low at the moment you feel you need to shop. You're not sure what it is, but your lethargy and fatigue propel you to the store to get some kind of relief. You seek out the stimulation the store can offer—colors, music, people—because you feel your life lacks luster and promise. Perhaps you experience other signs of depression, such as insomnia, weight gain or loss, or substance abuse.

8. You shop due to a perceived loss of control. Perhaps you've never conceptualized what it feels like *not* to shop compulsively. One person reported that she thought credit card debt was a way of life. Upon getting close to a man with financial savvy, she was astounded to learn that she could actively get herself out of debt and feel good about it. She learned that she was able to manage her finances. She began to set financial goals and enjoy the process. She even enjoyed balancing her checkbook, a project she never thought possible until opening herself up to the possibility of saving rather than spending. Don't forget that feeling out of control is a typical addictive behavior, like drinking, drugs, or gambling. Your addictions always seem to *control you*, but in reality, it is you who have given up control. A major emphasis of this book is to help you gain control over the anxiety that you feel, so that in the long run you are holding the reins of your life. You will move away from being a victim of your behavior, to being a person who understands and chooses a different path.

These eight descriptions are a way to help you begin categorizing your tendencies. You may notice some resistance in yourself at first. You may find yourself repeating rationalizations like "Well, it's on sale—I shouldn't pass it up," or "It's so pretty...I really *want* it," or "I might need it later." These are phrases that obscure the potential underlying motives you are trying to avoid. The next step is for you to become familiar with what motivates your shopping behavior.

Connect with Your Feelings

At this point you will find it useful to connect with the feelings surrounding each shopping venture. Feelings can be both emotional and physical. When you first notice the urge to shop, your body may physically react in an effort to express some hidden emotion. It may tense up, and your muscles become tight. You may feel sick, have headaches, or perhaps feel short of breath.

Let what happens to your body be a sign that something could be wrong. Pay attention to it. One way to do this is to sit down and allow yourself to become quiet for a moment. You may find it helpful to practice relaxation exercises—particularly helpful are deep-breathing exercises, progressive muscle relaxation, or autogentic phrases combined with imagery and positive self-talk. You'll find more in-depth descriptions of these techniques in chapter 7.

At first you may feel uncomfortable while focusing inward to relax, especially when the urge to shop strikes. Some people experience feelings of heaviness, drowsiness, or extreme anxiety because they are uncovering the possible motives driving them to shop. If this happens to you, tell yourself that these feelings are a natural part of any recovery effort. This flood of feelings has been lurking inside of you; you just haven't seen them because you turned to shopping as a quick way to dispel or suppress them. Eventually you won't have to shop to make these feelings go away; it just may take a bit longer for them to subside. Try to allow your feelings to flow through you and out of your body. You can also tell yourself that you will allow only a certain amount of feeling to surface at any given time, thereby controlling the amount of anxiety you feel.

If you are currently undergoing therapy for any reason, it is advisable for you to stay in close contact with your therapist, sharing with him or her any sensations or difficulties you experience as a result of practicing these exercises.

If your body doesn't seem to be telling you anything—that is, you don't notice any particular sensations—focus instead on any emotions you may be experiencing at the time of your urge. Some people report that they feel an overwhelming sadness and that their first desire is to ignore it by running off to the store. Others report rage or confusion. Becoming aware of these feelings is the necessary first step in getting control of your habit. Do not be afraid of them. Rather, allow them to surface and observe them curiously. You'll find more about this in chapter 6, where you'll be encouraged to adopt a stance of curiosity and objectivity. This approach to understanding your shopping problem can help you sift through and isolate the various emotions which may be steering you to shop.

A Visualization

If you feel stuck getting in touch with any physical sensations and emotions surrounding your shopping habits, sometimes doing a visualization can help.

A visualization is an imaginary scene that you create in your mind to help you reexperience and examine a problem area in your life. You can also use visualizations simply to help you relax and experience scenes of happiness and contentment. People use visualizations, also known as imagery, to aid recovery from serious illness, to set goals, and to reduce stress, among other things.

To do a visualization about shopping, you will first need to get comfortable. Put yourself in a quiet place, one where you will not be interrupted for at least twenty to thirty minutes. Practicing relaxation exercises for a few minutes at the start of your visualization period will help you focus and get in the mood. If you're not sure where to start, you can use the following suggested visualization script.

Remembering My Last Shopping Venture

I allow myself to see the scene. I'm walking toward the store. Where am I? What kind of store is it? What am I thinking as I approach the store? What am I feeling?

I enter the store. What time of day is it? Am I with someone? Is the store crowded? Who's around me?

What am I looking at to buy? I touch it. What does it feel like? What kinds of thoughts do I have as I touch it? What kinds of feelings do I have?

I pick it up and take it to the sales counter. I find my money or checkbook or credit card. As I pay for it I notice my thoughts. What are they? What do I feel?

I walk out of the store. I am feeling....

If you have trouble re-creating this scene or you feel silly attempting it, don't worry. Sometimes it takes several tries to allow yourself to have this imaginary conversation.

As soon as you complete your scene, jot down a few notes. What feelings emerged from this visualization? Did you notice a predominant pattern of thoughts you had? List both your thoughts and your feelings each time you do a visualization about shopping, so that you can preserve a running commentary on your habits. If you like, now would be a good time to convert a blank notebook to a shopping journal.

By participating in this visualization exercise, you've actually begun to assess your behavior. You are now ready to move on to the next chapter, "Keeping Track of Shopping Behaviors," a chapter which helps you pick apart your shopping behavior in order to get a handle on it.

5

Keeping Track of Shopping Behaviors

References in the current addiction literature to compulsive shopping suggest treatment plans similar to those for any addiction or compulsion. Of course, it's easy to define the parameters of abstinence for alcohol and drugs: you simply don't drink or use those substances any longer. While deciding never to shop again would give you a comparable method of gaining control over your addiction, that approach is clearly unrealistic. Just as compulsive eaters have to find a way of coping with the presence of food in their lives, you'll need to come to terms with some kind of shopping environment—if only in the form of your neighborhood grocery store. What will you do if you're called upon to buy a gift for someone? Or if you're forced to replace your washing machine when it finally breaks down and can't be repaired?

Some people overcompensate when they first attempt to control a bad habit—they jump off the deep end and make a desperate commitment to totally unrealistic demands, thinking that they will "lick" the habit once and for all. In effect, they approach the problem in a compulsive manner—they must do it perfectly, right away. (What else can you expect? People who shop compulsively will often try to replace their habits compulsively!) In the end, this less-than-gradual approach does not meet their expectations—they've demanded too much of themselves too soon—and they fail. Rather than set yourself up for failure, it is wisest to approach your problem gradually, with a plan—a plan that will help guarantee your success. In this chapter you will lay the groundwork for a plan that will work for you.

The first step is to become thoroughly familiar with your own unique shopping patterns. What cues you to buy something? Are you aware of your surroundings at the time? What are you feeling and thinking? What are the predictable consequences of each shopping venture?

Mapping out these specifics takes time and keen self-attention. The balance of this chapter involves focusing your attention on just such details. You'll uncover the situations, thoughts, feelings, and results—short term and long term—that characterize and perpetuate your shopping habit. This knowledge is the key to insight and recovery.

Record keeping is an important part of this journey to self-discovery. You'll find sample records here, as well as blank forms to fill in. Many people find it helpful to keep a personal journal as they work to change old habits. In your journal, you can record thoughts, frustrations, and successes with your shopping recovery program. You can attach copies of the assessment forms included here (perhaps in a notebook with folder pockets) or customize your own forms. Ideally, the journal will be compact enough to carry around with you. That way you'll be able to jot down feelings and urges as they occur—and also to take a moment, anywhere, to look over and reflect on what you've been doing.

You may be surprised at the power of a journal to capture patterns you never noticed before. In addition to recognizing particular cues and experiences that characterize your habit, you may also come to see an overall shape to your addiction. Most habits have an ebb and a flow, and it helps to realize that some days feel more difficult than others. Finally, a journal can be a treasured private space for musing and complaining about anything that happens (or doesn't happen) in the course of your day.

This chapter ends by suggesting you take time to work on your record keeping. If you give yourself about two weeks to pay attention to and take note of all your shopping habits, you'll find you have plenty of material to examine for clues into your behavior. The next chapter will help you sift through these notes to find the golden nuggets of insight that will lead to your recovery. Finally, at the end of chapter 6, you'll have a chance to develop a contract with yourself by setting goals and check-in points. In effect you'll create a "shopping list" that will help you get through the tough moments and stick to your goals.

This chapter and the one that follows are about figuring out where you are, how far you have to go, and making a plan and a resolution to get there. See it as an adventure—with a treasure of self-wisdom and strength awaiting you at the end.

Developing Your Shopping Record

Shoppers experience so many impressions and feelings with each shopping venture that it can be overwhelming to try to capture them all. Merely identifying your shopping cues—those little pokes and prods that encourage you to "fix" a situation by shopping—can be hard. And yet this is precisely the information you will need to understand the dimensions of your habit and tailor a plan for recovery.

The form that follows is your Shopping Record, designed to help you organize the jumbled thoughts, feelings, and actions of a typical shopping experience. The form has three parts: "Before," "During," and "After." This division recognizes the fact that each shopping experience has many sides to it—from the initial cue to shop, through the changing thoughts and feelings as you shop, to all the consequences of the trip, now and later. You'll find room for recording this information as it develops, whatever course of action you may choose on each separate occasion.

The Shopping Record looks like quite a bit of work, and it is. No one said that stopping the shopping habit was going to be easy. The advantage of the Record is that it organizes all the information most vital to your own recovery and puts it at your fingertips. Take a leap of faith right now and resolve to turn your full attention to completing several days worth of Shopping Records. The more you put in, the more you're guaranteed to get out.

To capture an accurate view of your habit, it is best to keep your record going for at least two weeks. (Before you begin, make as many blank copies of the form as you think you may need.)

Take a moment now to look through the forms. Later in this chapter, you'll have a chance to consider in greater detail the information requested in each question. After you've read through the chapter once, you'll be ready to begin.

Shopping Record

*(** Make copies of this form **)*

Date: _____

Part I. Before

To be completed as soon as you feel the urge to shop.

Situation:

1. Where am I?

2. What time is it?

3. Who am I with?

4. What am I doing? (Watching TV? Waiting for someone? Getting the mail?)

5. What just happened? (What recent event might be affecting me?)

6. Have I seen anything that might have triggered the urge to shop?

7. What other senses am I aware of? (What can I hear, smell, taste, feel?)

Urgency:

8. On this scale, draw an arrow that points to the number which best corresponds to your sense of urgency. For example, "0" would indicate no urgency whatsoever; "10" would indicate extreme urgency—you are unable to resist the urge to buy.

| 0 | 1 | 2 | 3 | 4 | 5 | 6 | 7 | 8 | 9 | 10 |

Thoughts:

9. What am I saying to myself right now that makes me want to shop?

10. What am I saying to myself that argues against shopping?

Feelings:

11. What physical sensations am I aware of right now? (A rapid heart rate? A stomachache? Do I feel cold? Are my palms sweating?)

12. What am I feeling emotionally? (Fearful? Anxious? Excited? A sudden calm? For more ideas, see the "Feelings List" at the end of this chapter.)

13. Do I have an unpleasant feeling that a purchase might make go away?

14. Is there a pleasant feeling that I think a purchase would give me?

Plan:

15. What do I plan to do now?

Part II. During

Complete Part A or Part B, depending on how you react to your shopping urge.

A. *If I Decide Not To Shop*

Right After the Decision:

1. What are my positive thoughts?

2. What are my negative thoughts?

3. What are my physical feelings?

4. What are my emotional feelings?

5. What am I doing?

One Hour Later:

6. What are my positive thoughts?

7. What are my negative thoughts?

8. What are my physical feelings ? (How have they changed?)

9. What are my emotional feelings? (How have they changed?)

10. How strong is my sense of urgency?

| 0 | 1 | 2 | 3 | 4 | 5 | 6 | 7 | 8 | 9 | 10 |

11. What am I doing?

That Night:

12. What did I do during the time I wasn't shopping?

13. When did the urgency pass or subside?

14. How do I feel now?

B. *If I Decide To Shop:*

Entering the Store/Filling in the Order Blank/Picking Up the Phone To Order:

1. What are my thoughts as I enter the shopping arena?

2. What are my physical feelings?

3. What are my emotional feelings?

4. What senses am I aware of? (Do I smell bread? See mannequins? Hear music?)

5. What do I do?

During a Shopping Break:

6. What exactly have I bought?

7. How much have I spent?

8. How did I or will I pay for these purchases?

9. What are my positive thoughts?

10. What are my negative thoughts?

11. What are my physical feelings? (How have they changed?)

12. What are my emotional feelings? (How have they changed?)

13. Will I continue to shop?

Final:

14. What else did I buy?

15. How much money did I spend, total?

16. How much time did I spend, total? (Include driving, shopping, unloading, and so on.)

Part III. After

Complete if you shopped.

When I Get Home or Stop Shopping:

1. What are my thoughts as soon as I return home or stop shopping?

2. What are my physical feelings?

3. What are my emotional feelings?

4. If my thoughts or feelings have changed, when did they?

5. What will I do with my purchases?

6. What work do I have to do to make up for the time I spent shopping?

Later:

7. What happens as a direct result of my shopping experience? (What activities do I do or miss? What conversations do I have or miss? What else?)

8. What happens when my spouse or domestic partner sees the purchases?

9. What happens in other relationships?

10. What are my thoughts about the shopping trip?

11. What are my feelings?

12. What happens when the bill comes?

13. Do I pay in full?

Ongoing:

14. What happens to the purchases? (How or when do I use them?)

15. What happens in my relationships?

16. What ongoing consequences are there from this shopping trip?

Keep this list going as new things come up: include any circumstances or consequences that you think might relate to your purchases or your shopping trip.

How To Use Your Shopping Record

When to write. To get the most out of your Shopping Record, it's best to fill in each section as close to the moment it asks about as possible. Obviously, you can't fill in the "Entering the Store" section as you step through swinging glass doors—but you can take a moment on a public bench or in the dressing room to note your impressions. You can also try memorizing your thoughts and feelings until you have a free moment to write, but be careful: you risk missing changes in your reactions and forgetting particular sensory details.

A shopping break is an important part of the "During" section. Later in this book, you'll learn to use this break to prevent potential needless purchases *before* they happen. For now, your job is simply to observe and to develop the habit of taking a break.

The "Before" section should be easy to fill out as soon as you're aware of your urge to shop. Adding notes to the "After" section should be an ongoing process for each shopping experience. Take a moment to write as soon as you get home and later that day or evening. But remember to keep going back to it as new consequences (bills, fights, compliments) unfold.

What it's asking for. Each question in the Shopping Record serves a purpose. In the next chapter, you'll have a chance to learn from your own answers to each question. For now, you may find it interesting to consider the thinking behind the questions a bit more carefully. That is the goal of the next section of this chapter.

More About the Questions

Part I. Before

Situation
Where am I?

Many people who shop compulsively find that they are particularly susceptible to shopping urges when they are in certain danger zones. For some people it's driving past the mall, for others it's sitting in front of the television set at home. One therapist who works with people with addictive tendencies uses the term "compulsive arena" to describe these danger zones. When you are in your compulsive arena, you may find yourself gripped by a sudden sense of urgency to shop. It can seem that only shopping will make the urgency go away.

If you experience a sense of urgency in a particular compulsive arena, pay particular attention to the urgency scale later in this section.

What time is it?

Everyone's body is tuned to a particular daily clock, called a "circadian rhythm." Some people are at their best first thing in the morning, and others feel that they come alive in the late afternoon, evening, or even at night. The times you become hungry, restless, sexually aroused, or sleepy can all be functions of your circadian rhythm. It follows that such strongly habitual behaviors as compulsive shopping may kick in at particular times of day, every day. Perhaps your shopping habit is tied to regular mood swings; then again, perhaps it is tied to a habitual activity that you do every day (such as pick up the mail). Be sure to note the time that the urge to shop first strikes.

Who am I with?

Yes, a person can be as much a cue to shop as a place or an advertisement. You can be influenced positively—for example, if you always shop with a favorite friend and find that buying things together enhances the friendship. You can also be influenced negatively—perhaps you envy certain people and want to emulate them or "show them up." You might shop to avoid certain people, or you may shop when you're alone and miss human company and interaction.

What am I doing?

Certain activities might lead you naturally to an urge to shop: watching TV, fighting with your spouse, beginning a project for work, doing nothing at all (and being bored), and so on. Your answer to this question may lead you to some insight about the underlying feeling produced by the activity and the role of your desire to replace (or avoid or extend) that feeling by shopping.

What just happened?

Allow yourself to think of every recent event that might be influencing you now. Think, too, about how those events may have affected your mood. Even if you can't see an immediate connection, you may find a pattern over time.

Have I seen anything that might have triggered the urge to shop?

Visual cues can be particularly effective triggers of desire. What are your eyes drawn to right now? Are there colors you associate with a particular mood, or displays or advertisements that tempt you? You may also be affected by *negative* visual cues—sights that you'd like to avoid or colors that depress you, perhaps.

What other senses am I aware of?

As you saw in chapter 3, all of your senses can be involved in your decision to shop. Run through your senses one at a time: sight, sound, touch, taste, smell. Which are you most aware of and how? Describe the sensual world around you in as much detail as possible.

Urgency

Placing a number value on this scale each time you sense an urge to shop will help you do several things. First, you'll gain a sense of "relative urgencies"—the knowledge that your urge to shop is not a constant force, but something that fluctuates with time and situation. What feels worse today may well feel better tomorrow. Second, once you can differentiate between urges, you'll be better able to see what may be behind them. Maybe the strongest urges always follow a particular mood or situation—which you can then plan to avoid or work to defuse. Finally, the scale will help you visualize your urgency, bringing it out in the open rather than keeping it buried deep within your feelings. In this way you can begin to see your urgency as something separate from you and downplay self-condemnation. When you condemn yourself, your thoughts, and your actions, it becomes harder for you to turn your energy to improvement.

In the next chapter, you'll find tips for managing urgencies of any strength. For now, concentrate on seeing and measuring the urgency as objectively as possible.

Thoughts

What am I saying to myself right now that makes me want to shop?

This question and the next ask you to focus on your self-talk. What you say to yourself has a powerful effect on your emotions and physical responses. Try to capture as exactly as possible the reasoning you are using to head out that door, pick up that phone, or fill in that order blank. What good will the specific purchase do you? How will the experience of shopping make you feel better?

What am I saying to myself that argues against shopping?

This is your rational voice. You may choose to ignore it, but chances are that on some level it is giving you a shopper-stopper sign. What are the words on that sign? Why should you not shop at this moment?

Feelings

What physical sensations am I aware of right now?

Throughout the process of record keeping and recovery, you will want to pay close attention to your body. It tells you a lot about yourself! Your first physical responses are your early warning system as you learn to combat the urge to shop. Does your heart rate speed up? Do your palms become sweaty? Many people find that their physical experience of urgency is similar to a stress response. Chapter 7 will teach you several methods for calming yourself when these feelings take hold. For now, do your best to tune in, recognize them, and name them.

What am I feeling emotionally?

The more specific you can be in naming your emotional state, the more success you will have in understanding your motivation to shop. One additional question to ask yourself is what other mood or emotion your current feelings resemble. You may find it helpful to refer to the list of feelings at the end of this chapter. Copy it and clip it in the back of your journal, if you like.

Do I have an unpleasant feeling that a purchase might make go away?

Here you deepen your search for clues about your true motivation to shop. Before you give way—or not—to a desire to distract yourself from, or compensate for, or completely avoid an unpleasant feeling, allow yourself to focus on it for a moment. How specifically can you name it? (And can you tie it to a particular recent event?)

Is there a pleasant feeling that I think a purchase would give me?

This is the positive side to the above question. It may be that the feeling you anticipate from shopping is a much stronger "reality" than the feeling or lack of feeling you experience now. Try, again, to name specifically the feeling that you hope to get from shopping. Eventually, this search for the underlying rewards of shopping will turn to a hunt for outlets other than shopping that give you the same pleasant feeling—chapter 8 provides plenty of ideas, when you're ready.

Plan

So, what will it be—to shop or not to shop? Be specific here, filling in the alternative to shopping if you decide not to shop or the exact itinerary if you decide to shop.

Part II. A. If I Decide Not To Shop

Right After the Decision

What are my positive thoughts?

Chances are the first few moments after you resolve not to give in to your habit will be the hardest, when the urgency to shop feels strongest. But you must be saying *some* positive, reinforcing things to yourself—or else you would have given in to the urge. Try to capture those thoughts as specifically as possible.

What are my negative thoughts?

Even if you fear your negative thoughts are "silly," try to write them down just as you hear them. Taking time to judge them only slows this process down. Are you addressing yourself directly? ("You'll just have to look like a slob at that party tomorrow.") Are you trying to suppress messages of fear? ("I may go crazy if I can't leave the house now, but I'll have to risk it.") What is your worst thought or fear about not shopping now? It can be hard to capture self-talk, since these messages tend to travel fast and hit their mark before you notice them passing. Work on slowing that thought process down to a pace that lets you hear the all-important messages in it.

What are my physical feelings?

Stay tuned into your bodily responses throughout your experience of resisting the urge to shop. Perhaps your stress response will remain high; perhaps your body will return quickly to normal, although you have the *sense* that you're in crisis. Later on you'll have a chance to see how these responses change over time. For now, record anything that feels slightly out of normal throughout your body at this moment.

What are my emotional feelings?

Again, try to label your emotional state, referring to the list at the end of this chapter as needed. If you come up with exactly the same word as before ("vulnerable" or "put-upon," for instance), try to register any difference in degree ("even more vulnerable," or "a little less put-upon, since I'm focusing on my own best interest now").

What am I doing?

Record exactly where you are and what activity you've engaged in. This will help you see later what activities have a positive effect on your mood and thoughts and which don't work at all to distract you from the discomfort of not shopping.

One Hour Later

Approach the same questions anew, one at a time. The important thing to learn is the progression of your thoughts and feelings—how they change, when they get better or worse, and what you can do to effect that change. You'll learn these answers after you've compiled a series of records. For now, focus on your state at the moment you answer the question.

That Night

This section gives you an opportunity to reflect on your entire experience of not shopping. Write down what you did with your time instead. Try to remember when the awful urgency to do your habit subsided and what you were doing at that time. Finally, write down all your negative and positive reactions to not shopping. What do you feel best about? What was the hardest part, and what helped it pass? How is your emotional and physical state right now? (Feel free to gloat about not shopping and feeling great about it, if you like!)

Part II. B. If I Decide To Shop

Entering the Store/Filling in the Order Blank/ Picking Up the Phone To Order

What are my thoughts as I enter the shopping arena?

Since your self-talk flows in a constant stream, it's best to stop and tune in at specific important moments. What you say to yourself when you first come within reach of your shopping reward may reveal something about that reward. For example, maybe you say, "Good—someone on the line." Maybe you say, "Whew, a familiar place where *I'm* running the show." Both statements point to underlying motivations to shop: social contact or control of one's environment. Listen, too, to the negative side of your self-talk. What thoughts make you uncomfortable as you begin to shop? Statements like "I can't afford to do this" or "Bob will kill me" are examples. The more precisely you can hear what you say, the more it stands to reveal about your underlying motivation to shop.

What are my physical feelings?

What you feel physically as you begin to shop can also reveal something of your reward in shopping. You may experience a tremendous release of tension as you give way to your habit—or you may feel a quickening of your pulse and a greater intensity of sensory perception. This information will be important when you begin to look for substitute activities that will get you to the same place. Make note of anything that feels out of the ordinary throughout your body.

What are my emotional feelings?

How do you feel about yourself and your life walking through that shop door? What is your dominant emotion now— and how does it differ from the one that sent you out shopping (from the "Before" section)? If it doesn't feel different, that's an important observation too. Perhaps you need some concentrated time in a shopping environment for the shopping "drug" to work for you. Write down whatever emotions are present. It may help you to look back at the self-talk you wrote down and recall how those thoughts made you feel.

What senses am I aware of?

Remember, each of your senses may be under assault in any shopping environment. Run through them one at a time: what can you see, hear, smell, taste, feel? Do any of these call up specific associations for you or lead you to move toward or away from their source? Take a moment to savor the sensory world around you.

What do I do?

Make note of the direction you're headed in—towards the shoes, back home, towards ordering more from the woman on the phone, to the fountain for a break, whatever. Answering this question will help you reflect for one more moment on your decision— and also remind you later what happened during this shopping trip.

During a Shopping Break

What exactly have I bought?

How much have I spent?

How did I or will I pay for these purchases?

All three questions above help you record precisely what you're doing now for your review later—and also give you a valuable moment to sit and reflect in the middle of your shopping expedition. It is all too easy to "turn off" your awareness of how much you're spending, what you're buying, and where you're going from one particular moment within a shopping binge to the next. These questions keep you aware of the facts. Perhaps you'll call it quits now, or perhaps you'll realize that your purchases are all rational and affordable. Before you begin to reflect, though, write down each item and price exactly.

What are my positive thoughts?

Once again, tune into your self-talk. In what ways do you feel good about your purchasing decisions? In what ways do you feel good about your plans to proceed from here? Be honest and precise.

What are my negative thoughts?

The critical voice within your head may be whispering messages of guilt; it may be screaming its head off that you can't afford your purchases and should beat it out of there; or it may be nowhere within hearing range. Try to pinpoint any negative messages you can. What are you saying to yourself that could make you feel bad?

What are my physical feelings? (How have they changed?)

How does the process of shopping continue to affect your bodily responses? Does shopping help calm you down or keep you excited? What particularly strong responses to triggers in your shopping environment do you recall? Did your heart skip a beat at a missed sale sign, or your palms sweat when your favorite salesclerk wasn't there to help? Scan your body for anything out of the ordinary and write it down.

What are my emotional feelings? (How have they changed?)

Continue to track your emotional ride through your shopping experience. Before looking back to your earlier notes, assess your emotional state at this moment. Once you have done so, look back to see how it's changed since you began shopping and try to elaborate. For instance, suppose you note that you feel "emotionally drained." You may have written "drained" in the "Before" section to describe your emotional state at home. It's valuable information if you can record that you feel "drained from the experience of shopping" now. That distinction might indicate to you, later, that the experience of shopping actually *replaced* the experience of home in your emotional awareness: distraction may have been your true goal.

Will I continue to shop?

Decide what you want to do, write it down, and do it. In chapter 9, "Fighting Back," you'll learn to use this shopping break as a way to weigh all of your purchases rationally before you make them. For this reason, the shopping break is an important habit to cultivate. At this stage of the game, however, it is enough to take a break simply to observe your thoughts, feelings, and plans. Consider yourself an objective observer of the habit within you.

Final

What else did I buy?
How much money did I spend, total?
How much time did I spend, total?

Record these facts as precisely as possible. As you'll learn in chapter 10, it is a good idea to write down every purchase you make and every dollar you spend. What's more, recording them in this fashion will help you find relationships between the amount you spend, your mood, the earliest triggers that gave rise to the shopping expedition, and more. Remember, no one need see this list but you—so you might as well be honest.

Part III. After

When I Get Home or Stop Shopping
What are my thoughts as soon as I return home or stop shopping?
What are my physical feelings?
What are my emotional feelings?

In this section, you continue to monitor the progression of your thoughts and your feelings. Chances are that neither will be the same as they were when you began to shop. Your job now is to record the changes as precisely as possible by focusing on the present moment. Find a new word for your emotional state (or use a relative term such as "a much-less-trapped feeling" to distinguish it from the trapped feeling you felt earlier). Find as accurate as possible a phrasing for your self-talk, both positive and negative.

If my thoughts or feelings have changed, when did they?

To the extent that you can pinpoint a moment when your feelings plunge, such as walking in and seeing last month's Visa bill on your desk, write it down exactly. Similarly, if you experience sudden elation at walking in with few or no new packages, try to capture that joy and that moment in words. These moments will serve as powerful memories and incentives later in your recovery program.

What will I do with my purchases?

Here, too, honesty counts. Account for each item you bought and record the specific details of what you plan to do with it, and when.

What work do I have to do to make up for the time I spent shopping?

The work you have to do to make up for your shopping trip can take a number of forms. You might have to do tasks or pay visits that you postponed in order to shop. You may have to readjust your budget or vow to skimp financially in other areas to make up for the amount you spent. Or you may have some explaining to do to others or yourself to account for your behavior. Include anything that comes to mind here, whether an actual task ("Still have to have Aunt Dorothy over for lunch") or a feeling ("I've got to live with this damn guilt now") or a resolution ("I have to work harder at moving forward in the book and not shopping").

Later
What happens as a direct result of my shopping experience?

Think of any immediate plans that changed. Did you miss an opportunity or come into new opportunities as a result of shopping? This question begins to cast the net wider for every possible consequence—and possible motivation—for shopping.

What happens when my spouse or domestic partner sees the purchases?

Describe the scene as precisely as you can: what he or she says, what you say, what each of you do. How does this affect your immediate relationship? What lingering effects are there throughout the day and evening? How does his or her reaction change—soften or grow worse—over time? Intimate relationships often have a great deal to do with habitual behavior and certainly with your fluctuating moods and experiences. Even if your spouse or partner does not know about your shopping experience, record what happens in your thoughts and feelings about the relationship that day or evening. (Perhaps you resent having to hide things; perhaps you feel guilty and work hard to be a pleasant companion; perhaps you make plans to leave; perhaps you seek reassurance.)

What happens in other relationships?

Who else is affected by your shopping experience, and how does your relationship change? Perhaps you become closer to the friend you shopped with; perhaps you fear that your compulsive collecting is making you more and more like your father and begin to distance yourself from both parents. This question, like the one above, will ultimately lead to a search for *rewards*. That is, perhaps you seek ways to become closer to that one friend or to distance yourself from your parents through shopping. Chances are that you can accomplish the same interpersonal goals—whether or not they seem like obvious goals to you—without resorting to shopping. For now, think about every relationship that was affected by and that might have something to do with your shopping behavior.

What are my thoughts about the shopping trip?

What are my feelings?

This is your space for a roundup of your self-talk and feelings. What are you saying to yourself and how are you feeling now? Answering those immediate questions will give you an end point to the continuum of your thoughts and feelings about today's shopping trip. Try also to look for an overview of your thoughts and feelings. Did shopping ultimately lift your spirits or depress you further? Are you feeling better about yourself or worse? Feel free to jot down whatever insights may occur to you about the role shopping played in affecting your overall mood or outlook.

What happens when the bill comes?

Approach this question from different perspectives. What happens financially—do you have enough to pay? Where do you take the money from? (What else might you have bought with it?) What happens emotionally—are you shocked, let down, numb, confused, or any other nameable emotion? What do you say to yourself—on the positive and the negative sides? If you hide the bill or put it onto one of many piles on your desk, write that fact down, too. It is important that you see the bill's arrival as an integral part of the shopping experience.

Do I pay in full?

Write down how much the bill is for and how much of it you pay. This will be helpful information over time.

Ongoing

This section of the Record can be filled in over the following days and even weeks after the shopping venture. Be sure you've marked the date and the items purchased on each new record so that you can refer back to it to keep adding to this section.

What happens to the purchases?

Account for each item you bought. Did you use them as you thought you would? Are you still waiting to use some—with specific future plans or without? Make a mark each time you wear a new pair of earrings or listen to a new CD, if you can. It might be instructive for you to average out the cost of any purchase on a per-use basis.

What happens in my relationships?

In what ways does the arrival of the bill affect any of your relationships? Consider an actual reaction to the bill (say, if your wife sees the cost of your new boots and explodes) as well as any repercussions of your own reaction (say, if it puts you in a sour mood, and you snap at the children). Does using the purchase (giving the present, wearing the new dress) affect any relationships? Write down whatever you can think of, positive or negative, even if you're not sure how the association is connected.

What ongoing consequences are there from this shopping trip?

Anything you can think of is fair game here. Include any opportunity, fight, insight, change in your thoughts or feelings about shopping—whatever you think might be related to this shopping trip or your entire habit, however indirectly.

Tips on Using Your Shopping Record

• Make a point of setting aside regular breaks throughout your shopping experience to write in your record. That break is important in itself. It gives you room to breathe and reflect as you step back to observe your behavior. (This kind of interruption is called a "time wedge.")

• Don't worry about big recovery plans or trying to control your shopping urges just yet. That comes later. It's enough to be honest and thorough in your observations.

• Watch out for negative self-talk as you fill in your Shopping Record, such as "This is stupid" or "I must look foolish" or "I'm really out of control." These kinds of disparaging statements only get in your way. You'll find it helpful if you allow yourself to adopt a stance of "inquiring" into the nature of your habit, without censoring or judging yourself. You can be a privileged observer, checking into your behavior and emotions with freedom to explore all avenues. Omitting any behavior because you find it embarrassing or inexplicable will only block your path to full recovery.

• Be sure to copy as many blank forms as you think you'll need before you begin. Insert them in the back of your journal if you think you can carry it everywhere with you or leave copies on your car seat, in your purse or briefcase, by the television—wherever they can be immediately accessible. As soon as you think you're reacting to a cue to shop, pull out a form and begin writing.

• You may choose to share your forms with a trusted other person. Many people find that a "recovery buddy" offers moral support and encouragement. If you decide this would be helpful, be sure to advise the person beforehand what you want from him or her. Just looking at the forms with you or spending time with you while you look them over may be enough. Ask your friend to remember that judgmental statements such as "You really went wild on Wednesday!" are seldom helpful. You may or may not want help from your buddy when you begin combing your forms for connections and clues into the nature of your habit.

• Collect these forms for at least two weeks. Any less might not give you a fair sample of behaviors. The more experiences you have to learn from and average out, the more accurate the material will be that you'll have to guide your recovery plans.

The information that you compile here will serve as the raw material for chapter 6, "Learning from Your Shopping Record." Based on your own observations, you will identify personal trouble spots and make plans to avoid them. You will also identify the deeper rewards that you get from shopping and learn how to attain them without blowing an entire paycheck. Chapter 6 will help you make short-term plans to cope with urgency attacks and set long-term goals to keep you focused on what you really want in life.

If you sense that you are having trouble putting your feelings into words, read over the following list of words describing feelings and see if any of them fit.

Feeling Words

affectionate	drained	infuriated	resentful
angry	eager	intimidated	sad
anxious	energetic	isolated	satisfied
betrayed	exasperated	jealous	scared
blissful	fearful	jumpy	shocked
blue	flustered	left-out	social
bored	foolish	lonely	spiteful
burdened	frantic	loving	stunned
charmed	frustrated	melancholy	stupid
cheated	funny	miserable	sympathetic
cheerful	generous	nervous	tense
condemned	grief-stricken	numb	terrible
confused	guilty	OK	terrified
contented	happy	outraged	tired
crushed	helpful	overworked	trapped
defeated	helpless	persecuted	troubled
deprived	high	pressured	ugly
despairing	horrible	put-upon	vulnerable
disoriented	hurt	rejected	weak
distraught	hysterical	relaxed	weepy
disturbed	ignored	relieved	wonderful
dominated	imposed-on	remorseful	worried

6

Learning from Your Shopping Record

If you have kept a Shopping Record diligently for two weeks, you now have a treasure trove of information about your unique shopping behavior. This chapter will present several ways for you to comb that record for facts vital to your recovery. At the end of this chapter, you'll have a chance to finalize your recovery goals in a contract to yourself.

To successfully complete this chapter, you will need:

- Your filled-in Shopping Records from chapter 5

- Colored pens or pencils

- A willingness to gain insight, and a desire for positive change

Recognizing Your Cues

Discovering the cues that trigger your shopping behavior is one main function of the "Before" section of the Shopping Record. A cue is the little voice in your head that tells you something is amiss. Perhaps you've never noticed such a voice. If you're not tuned in to an inner voice, a cue can take on many other forms, such as a gnawing, anxious feeling in the pit of your stomach, rapid breathing, heart pounding, or simply the vague feeling that something isn't right. A cue can even be a time of day or a particular activity.

Situational Cues

Look over the "Situation" section now from part I of your Shopping Records. Is there a typical time of day when the urge to shop strikes? A particular event? Were you frequently spending time with a particular person? The "Situation" section may also reveal sensory cues: things you saw, heard, smelled, tasted, or touched. Do you recognize a theme here?

Use this space to record cues that you think may be important. Skip any lines that you don't find relevant or use the extra space to continue your thoughts from another line.

1. I tend to shop when I am at these places:_____

   _____

2. I tend to shop at this time of day:_____

   _____

3. I tend to shop when I am with these people:_____

   _____

4. I tend to shop after I_____

   _____

5. Seeing this triggers an urge to shop: _____

   _____

6. These sensory impressions trigger an urge to shop: _____

   _____

Dealing with Situational Cues

The best way to deal with situational cues is to avoid them. Stay out of your "compulsive arena." Try not to be available when your shopping buddy is ready to shop (suggest a movie instead). Make plans for your dangerous time of day. To the extent that you can stay away from the people, places, and things that trigger your shopping urge, you will retain greater control and resolve over your habit.

Obviously you can't avoid all your cues. When you must visit a shopping area that tempts you or find yourself within a powerful blast of warm, sweet air from the bakery, be on the alert. Acknowledge to yourself that you are in the presence of strong shopping cues and enact as many coping mechanisms as you can. Later chapters will teach you specific coping skills for various shopping danger cues: chapter 7 will help you fight anxiety and stress, for instance, and chapter 9 will help you resist advertisements, malls, catalogs, and so on. For now, though, you can begin to plan alternative behaviors.

The real trick in planning alternative behaviors is to choose something you truly enjoy. If you find alternatives that are at least a little bit rewarding and in line with your general well-being and health, you will feel *rewarded* by not shopping, instead of deprived. For example, one woman put herself on a diet while she was learning to manage her shopping addiction. One alternative she chose was walking to the frozen yogurt store whenever she felt the urge to shop. The yogurt was better for her than her expensive purchases and in line with her health-conscious goals (she ate only the nonfat variety). Since the yogurt felt like a reward after the walk, she also felt fulfilled by the experience.

The Alternative Behaviors Form on the following page is your space to work out activities you feel you would truly enjoy. Feel free to refer to chapter 8, "Alternatives to Shopping: From A-Z," for more ideas, and keep the list going as more alternatives come to mind. Post the list on your refrigerator door, in your car, or wherever you will spot it easily. Be as specific and honest as possible about your situational cues and your alternatives—the more specific, the better.

Alternative Behaviors Form

Place cue. When I am at _____
and experience an urge to spend, I can choose to do these alternative behaviors:

1. _____

2. _____

3. _____

Thing cue. When I see _____
and experience an urge to spend, I can choose to do these alternative behaviors:

1. _____

2. _____

3. _____

Person cue. When I am with_____

or when I see _____
and experience an urge to spend, I can choose to do these alternative behaviors:

1. _____

2. _____

3. _____

Emotional and physical cues. When I feel _____
and experience an urge to spend, I can choose to do these alternative behaviors:

1. _____

2. _____

3. _____

Thoughts

As you may have realized while filling out your Shopping Record, cues can also take the form of thoughts and feelings. Take a look at the "Thoughts" section of part I. The Record divides persuasive thoughts *for* shopping from persuasive thoughts against. It's time now to identify the strongest arguments on each side, beginning with those you give yourself for shopping. Rely on what you wrote about each thought in your Shopping Record, as well as on your intuitive sense of which argument had the greatest effect on your subsequent decision to shop. In the space below, list those most persuasive arguments.

Persuasive Thoughts for Shopping

Example: I worked so hard this week, I deserve to go out and buy a new dress.

1. _____

2. _____

3. _____

4. _____

5. _____

6. _____

Dealing with Thoughts

Look carefully at each of these arguments to shop. Chances are that some seem more realistic, more logically true, than others. Ask yourself now which arguments seem believable to you and which seem questionable. Take out your colored pencils, and underline the believable arguments with one color and questionable ones with another.

For instance, the thought that you need a new outfit for a party because you are pregnant and nothing you own will fit is a sound argument to shop. The thought that you need a new outfit because your sister is pregnant and you want to stand out at her baby shower is not quite as sound. The second argument sounds like an excuse; the first like legitimate need. Getting a new set of screwdrivers in order to finish a bookcase project sounds like a reasonable decision. Buying a set of expensive tools because you saw the guy use a similar set on the fix-it show on TV sounds less reasonable. Separating believable thinking from questionable thinking is much easier to do when you step back, out of the rush of the habit. Look over your list now and be sure you've marked each argument believable or questionable.

Each believable reason to shop serves as its own justification—you don't need to explore it further since you went shopping for a valid reason on that occasion. (Make sure, though, that the reason you gave yourself wasn't covering deeper feelings. If so, you'll want to put those feelings into words.) Each questionable argument, however, should be explored and refuted.

The space below is yours to use to question your justifications for shopping when there is no logical reason to shop. In the first column, list the reason you gave yourself to justify shopping. In the second column, argue as persuasively as you can against the reasoning in the first column. Rely on facts and ideas you know to be true; phrase your arguments so you will believe them. You get to be the attorney for your own prosecution (and defense!).

Answers to Arguments for Shopping

Argument	*Answer*
Example: I worked so hard this week, I deserve to buy a new dress.	*I deserve a better reward than just a new thing! I deserve to be unworried, relaxed, and in control of my finances. I deserve to relax without spending a dime today.*

1. _____   _____

_____   _____

_____   _____

2. _____   _____

   _____   _____

   _____   _____

3. _____   _____

   _____   _____

   _____   _____

For further practice in turning negative, destructive thinking into positive and realistic thoughts, see "Refuting Irrational Ideas" in chapter 7.

Building a Resistance List

The second column in the form above is the beginning of your Resistance List to shopping. You'll keep your Resistance List in your journal, your pocketbook, or anywhere that it will be easily accessible when you feel a dangerous urge to shop. Start a new page in your journal now, or take a clean sheet of paper to add into it, and copy over the best answers from the second column above. Each of these arguments should be a thought *you know to be true* that will remind you to think and not to shop when you feel the urge to lose control. If you use your own words and best powers of persuasion for every item on the list, you'll have a powerful tool at your disposal.

The Resistance List is something you can keep going as you come up with more arguments and insights against shopping. Later sections in this chapter will help you add to it. Just remember, for almost every argument to shop, there is an equally powerful argument not to shop. Use your creativity and wisdom to find it.

To continue building your Resistance List, look now to question 10 on part I of your Shopping Record: "What am I saying to myself that argues *against* shopping?" Also look at part III, consequences of the shopping trip. What happens as a direct result (question 7), what are the ongoing consequences (question 16), what happens to your relationships (questions 9 and 15), what happens when the bill comes (questions 12 and 13)? Select the strong-est arguments from those entries and underline those in a new color. Take a moment to consider each of those arguments, and ask yourself how you can build its strength, making it even more per-suasive. For instance, suppose you wrote: "I'll faint when I see the bill if I get those new speakers." Add to it: "I'll revive and faint again each month as the finance charges add up. I'll probably enter a coma when I can't pay the minimum amount and they take the card and the stereo away." It's okay to exaggerate a bit if the effect is to remind you of a reasonable danger.

Use the space below to list your best arguments against shopping, and to build those arguments even further in strength and persuasiveness.

Persuasive Thoughts Against Shopping

Original Thought

Addition

Example: Bob will divorce me if I buy another pair of shoes.

Bob will divorce me, and I'll feel like divorcing myself.

1. _____   _____

_____   _____

_____   _____

2. _____   _____

_____   _____

_____   _____

3. _____   _____

_____   _____

_____   _____

Copy the most persuasive arguments above into your Resis-tance List. Ideally, the list should provide as much inspiration as castigation—calling attention to the rewards of not shopping, as much as the costs of shopping. Your Resistance List should now contain the arguments from both columns above, and from the "Answers to Arguments for Shopping" list earlier.

Physical Feelings

Sometimes a certain physical feeling, such as stress, can lead to a desire to shop for relief. Sometimes it goes the other way, and the desire to shop can give way to telltale physical responses— shallow, rapid breathing or a pounding heart. Either way, those physical cues spell danger to the compulsive shopper. Learning to recognize your typical physical responses before a shopping expedition can help keep you aware.

What physical reactions serve as your cues to shop? Look over your response to question 11 on part I of all of your Shopping Records.

My typical physical cues to shop are: _____

_____

_____

_____

Dealing with Physical Feelings

What else might you do to relieve these negative feelings or produce these positive feelings other than shop? This is an area that will be explored in greater depth in chapter 7, "Anxiety and Stress Relief," as well as in chapter 8, "Alternatives to Shopping: From A to Z." Chances are you have some ideas already. The more you can anticipate these feelings in advance and plan your reactions, the better off you'll be.

You'll also want to examine how your physical response changes over time: does shopping make the feeling go away or does it increase it? (Look particularly at your responses to questions 3 and 8 of part II.) Pay special attention to the positive feelings associated with shopping. Ultimately, you'll want to achieve this same positive feeling that shopping offers—a "high," or the disappearance of a stomachache, without resorting to shopping. Does shopping excite you or calm you? Once you learn to find these kinds of rewarding feelings in pursuits that don't involve shopping, you're well on your way to freedom from your habit. That is, something *else* may excite you or calm you even better—in the short and long term.

For now, you'll want to take any negative feelings associated with shopping seriously. If shopping always gives you a headache, add this fact to your Resistance List. You may forget that when the urge strikes, but the memory of a shopping headache can be enough to keep you home one day.

Consider, too, what happens to your physical feelings if you decide *not* to shop. This area will be particularly helpful when you consider the section of the Shopping Record dealing with your sense of urgency. The way your feelings actually progress may not be the way you predict they will progress if you refrain from shopping.

Emotions

One of the hardest tasks in human communication can be finding the right word for a specific emotion. Rather than occupying one small unit of your awareness—one word's worth of your brainspace—your emotional state at any given moment colors everything you do, see, and think. No wonder that people talk about "feeling blue," "seeing red," and being "green with envy."

Very often, addictive behavior is triggered by the urge to flee a particularly difficult emotion—depression, anxiety, helplessness, despair. Perhaps you've experienced such an urge for escape before a shopping binge and can recognize how shopping distracts you or lets you numb yourself. If not, let yourself explore the idea that a similar dynamic works at a less-than-conscious level for you and that you shop to escape emotions you're not fully aware of. Allow yourself to consider the possibility, for the length of this section, that negative emotions do fuel your urge to shop.

Your Shopping Record afforded many opportunities for you to record your emotional state before, during, and after shopping. Whether or not you referred to the list of feelings at the end of chapter 5, you probably used a wide range of words to describe your feelings at any particular moment. Such a list can help you recognize an emotion as you're feeling it (or at least part of an emotion). In the section that follows, you will learn to recognize the larger emotion that may be reflected by the specific words that you wrote down. From there, you can begin to plan exactly what you are going to do instead of shopping when you start feeling sad, bored, anxious, and so on. As soon as a familiar feeling like boredom steals over you and you think about heading for the mall, you will instead remember your planned alternative behavior and go for a walk or call a friend. When you realize that you're nervous about an upcoming appointment, that will be your signal to do relaxation exercises rather than shop.

Read carefully through the following list and check off or underline the feelings that trigger shopping for you, the real needs that you seem to be trying to meet, and any of the suggested alternative behaviors that appeal to you. Use the extra spaces to add alternative behaviors better suited to your individual interests, situation, and abilities.

Feelings that Trigger Shopping	Real Needs	Alternative Behaviors To Meet Needs
lonely alone abandoned	companionship belonging inclusion	call a friend visit somebody get a pet go to a club meeting take a class go to singles group

sad
depressed
sense of loss
	happiness
	hope
	meaning
		tell best friend about it
		go jogging
		plan favorite amusement
		plan a weekend away
		do something for
		    someone you love
		build something
		list my strengths and
		    assets as a person

anxious
scared
frightened
nervous
	relaxation
	stress reduction
	safety
		progressive muscle
		    relaxation
		deep breathing
		share feelings with
		    someone
		vigorous exercise
		listen to music

bored restless	activity interest	practice piano take a walk rearrange furniture, desk, kitchen drawers go to a movie rent a video

Feelings that Trigger Shopping	Real Needs	Alternative Behaviors To Meet Needs
		go to zoo (amusement park, museum)
		go for a drive
tired	rest	take a nap
fatigued	relaxation	read
worn out		postpone commitments
		watch a video, or some passive entertainment
		listen to music
empty	reward	treat yourself to a good meal
yearning	acknowledgment	cut some flowers from garden
emotionally hungry	satisfy emptiness	review past successes
		have hair done
		join a group activity that meets regularly
		ask for support with a problem
		arrange a visit with a friend
angry	to be heard	use problem solving together
resentful	asserting rights	express pain openly
frustrated	revenge	hit a pillow
		confront lover with concerns

Feelings that Trigger Shopping	Real Needs	Alternative Behaviors To Meet Needs

unloved
unworthy
	self-worth
	to be loved
	re-experience
	    mother's love
		hug someone
		cuddle and kiss
		tell someone "I love you"
		make love
		use self-acceptance
		    affirmations

guilty
bad
wrong
undeserving
	forgiveness
	atonement
	punishment
		plan atonement
		use "I am only human/I
		    forgive myself"
		    affirmations
		donate your money to
		    charity
		do volunteer work
		remind myself that past
		    actions are over and
		    done with

oppressed
discriminated
    against
	equality
	asserting rights
		join support group
		write a letter of protest
		talk it over with a
		    like-minded friend
		speak up to challenge
		    unfair treatment

hurt
criticized
unappreciated
	recognition
	appreciation
		tell about your hurt
		    without blaming
		ask for what you want
		    assertively

Feelings that Trigger Shopping	Real Needs	Alternative Behaviors To Meet Needs
_____	_____	_____
_____	_____	_____
_____	_____	_____
_____	_____	_____
_____	_____	_____
_____	_____	_____
_____	_____	_____
_____	_____	_____

Spend plenty of time on this exercise, until you have clearly identified the feelings that drive you into the mall, the real needs you are trying to fill, and some good alternative behaviors you can perform to fill these needs. Use this list to make up affirmation cards in this format:

When I feel (feeling that triggers shopping),
I fill my need for (real need)
by (alternative behavior)
or (second alternative behavior)
instead of shopping.

Be as specific as possible in describing what you will do. Instead of writing "Go for a walk," write "Walk down to the lake and feed the ducks." Notice that you should have at least two alternative behaviors planned, to increase your options and be prepared for different circumstances.

This exercise was adapted from *Lifetime Weight Control*, by Patrick Fanning (Oakland, CA: New Harbinger Publications, 1990).

Urgency

The sudden urgency you may feel at times to do your habit can feel like a wave crashing down on you, sweeping away all your resolution to refrain from shopping, and dragging you out to sea. This can be the most frustrating and frightening moment in quitting a habit.

But while urgency can seem all-powerful and overwhelming when it hits, your Shopping Record reveals a larger pattern in the urgency you feel. Look back at your forms now and see if you can complete the following "noticing" exercise.

Notice the fact that high urgency always passes—whether you shop or not. Can you find an example of urgency when you decided not to shop? How did that feeling change with time? How long did it take to change? How did it compare to times when you *did* shop?

Knowing an approximate time frame—whether it will take an hour or ten minutes or half a day—can help you to see an end in sight when the urgency first hits.

Notice how your urgency changes from one incident to the next. On one day the urge to shop may feel like a "9," and on another day a "4." What is your range? Can you see factors that might have contributed to lower or higher urgency?

Recognizing the fact that urgencies change with time can help you see the feeling not as a tidal wave, but as a regular wave with a manageable ebb and a flow. People suffering chronic pain— from backaches, injury, and illness—report that recording relative strengths in pain helps them recognize that they are not always simply "in pain," but that some moments are easier than others. The fact that something feels worse today means that there's plenty of reason to believe it will feel better tomorrow.

Notice the cues, arguments, and feelings that led to your strongest sense of urgency. These arguments to shop are likely to hold deeper meaning for you. Ask yourself what similarities you see among the cues, arguments, and feelings in the three records that you ranked the most urgent. Use the space that follows to help sort your thoughts and findings.

High Urgency Factors

A. What were my situational cues (people, places, events)?

Time 1. _____

Time 2. _____

Time 3. _____

B. What were my arguments for shopping?

Time 1. _____

Time 2. _____

Time 3. _____

C. What was I feeling emotionally?

Time 1. _____

Time 2. _____

Time 3. _____

If you haven't already addressed these cues and feelings in the earlier sections, take a moment now to add them to your list of cues to avoid or to plan alternatives for. What alternative activities do you think might have helped? What answers can you come up with for these persuasive arguments to shop? (Add those to your Resistance List!)

Finally, notice opportunities for insight into the deepest reasons for your shopping problem. What can you learn about yourself from the feelings you listed above? Chances are these are the feelings closest to the root of your shopping problem. Ask yourself whether you can think of constructive alternatives to these feelings. Imagine how you might have dealt with each feeling more directly, instead of releasing, escaping, or avoiding it through shopping.

Dealing with Urgency When It Hits

When the urge to shop first strikes, focus on the image of urgency as a wave—a wave that will pass if you can just ride it out. Keep this image firmly in your mind. Meanwhile, rely on any or all of the tips below to keep yourself afloat:

- Tell yourself that the urgency is a force outside you that will pass.

- Pull out old Shopping Records and *see* that the urgency has always passed.

- Pull out your Resistance List. Tell yourself every good argument against shopping.

- Call a trusted friend or counselor. Describe what is going on and explain that you need help riding this feeling out.

- Look at the consequences of other shopping trips. Visualize all the negative consequences now (imagine a fight with your spouse or picture the utility money subtracted from your checkbook with the bill still due). Recall the ill feeling of returning from a shopping trip by reading about it now.

- Engage in one of the activities from your Alternative Behaviors Form at the beginning of this chapter.

Chapter 11, "When the Going Gets Tough," offers a few more ideas for toughing it out. At this stage of the game, however, you are already well-armed to combat your own worst instincts.

Looking for Connections

Your Shopping Record contains many more insights into your shopping behavior, your needs, your patterns of thinking, and your underlying motivations to shop. The more time you're willing to spend going over your forms—and, in fact, filling out your forms thoroughly—the more wisdom you stand to glean about yourself. Every new insight you gain is valuable in itself and also rich in its promise to help you change your current behavior and address your frustrations.

The following guide can help you to organize your continuing examination of your Shopping Record. If you'd like to use these items as a simple reflective exercise, that's fine. Or, if you still have sharp pencils in unexplored colors and you're feeling inspired, feel free to draw connecting lines and dots between items that seem related.

Look for connections between the urgency of your need to shop and the amount you spend. How much does your initial impulse to shop affect your subsequent shopping experience? Does the strength of the urgency affect how "in control" you feel once you begin to shop, or does it just serve to get you out the door? Recognizing patterns here might help you plan a course of action when you feel an urge of a particular intensity.

Look for connections between the amount you spend and how you feel afterward. Do you feel better the more you spend, or does spending more lead to greater feelings of guilt and despair? The answer to this question can point to whether you rely on purchases themselves to feel better, or whether it's the experience of shopping that matters, regardless of the things bought. It can also tell you whether shopping touches your underlying feelings at all, or whether you've simply avoided those feelings by distracting yourself with shopping.

Look for connections between your thoughts and your feelings. Chapter 7, "Anxiety and Stress Relief," will explore in greater depth the connection between thoughts—what you say to yourself—and feelings. Basically, a lightning-fast thought almost always precedes a change in emotion. Can you see any links between what you said to yourself in questions 9 and 10 of part I and the feelings you noted in questions 12 through 14? Or between thoughts and feelings you recorded in part II, during shopping? The Shopping Record is organized so that you always note your thoughts before you note your feelings. Tracing connections between specific thoughts and corresponding feelings is a crucial step in getting a handle on destructive emotions: by changing what you say to yourself, you can change your emotional reactions.

Look for connections between people, places, and things, and your behavior. Your search for situational cues to shop should be ongoing. Are there particular people who arouse your envy every time you see them? Or people who cool your desire to buy and help you feel more spiritually secure? Keep a constant eye out for external factors that influence your shopping behavior—and learn to eliminate those cues you find most troublesome.

Look for connections between shopping and the rest of your life. Does what you do when you shop remind you of your behavior in any other area of your life? Does it remind you of yourself at a particular time in your life—childhood, adolescence, young adulthood, or a period dominated by a particular emotion, such as hope, depression, fear, or love? What might you be searching for or trying to make up for or re-creating in your persistent shopping? Give yourself some freedom to explore the depths and shape of your shopping habit. If you find that you tap into deep wells of emotion—or if you feel that there is meaning there that you just can't tap—you might consider continuing your exploration with the help of a professional counselor.

Making a Plan

A woman who suffered for years from compulsive shopping (but didn't know it) finally sought some help. Jane and her counselor set goals and developed a plan. To begin with, she got a dog from the SPCA. The dog required time and attention, and when Jane felt the urge to spend money she could always walk the dog. Since you can't take a dog into most stores, it helped her avoid the temptation of shopping on their walks—which gave Jane exercise, too. Jane also resolved to give away five items per week (she had been hoarding her purchases). She went on to put her compulsive tendencies to work for her by starting on a complicated, calorie-counting weight-loss program and by signing up for those golf and tennis lessons that she had "never had the time for" before. Since she was channeling her compulsions toward more healthy pursuits, she began to feel better about herself. As a pleasant and unexpected result, she met someone and got involved in a rewarding relationship.

Basically Jane was learning self-management. To start out, she enlisted the support of others at work and at home (including a friend who agreed to come over every few days and throw out the catalogs which consistently filled Jane's mailbox. Eventually Jane was able to do this for herself). Most importantly, Jane was learning the cues that warned her when she was in a compulsive arena, so that she would be able to prevent the problem from snowballing again. Whenever she recognized that urgent sense that she just had to buy something, she would insert a time-wedge at that point—something else to do to get through the urge.

In tandem with her behavioral management program, Jane was able to gain emotional insight into her behavior through counseling. She began to understand the connection between money and affection, which she had made during her late childhood and early teen years. Her parents had divorced; her father had developed another relationship, which took him away on weekends. She guessed that out of his own guilt in leaving her alone, he'd give her his credit card to use freely. In other words, she came to learn at an early age that money and spending were symbols of love and affection. She had carried this unconscious assocation into her adult life by buying gifts for people as compulsively as she shopped for herself. As she progressed through her counseling and behavioral management program, she learned that she could manage potential relapses by increasing her contact with other people, thereby decreasing her feelings of isolation and deprivation.

Your Self-Contract

In his book *The Addictive Personality*, Craig Nakken outlines a step-by-step process of recovery from any habit. One of the most important steps is to "define abstinence in recovery." In other words, you need to spell out exactly what the addictive behavior is that you wish to avoid. Can you window-shop and not commit shopping? Or will window-shopping increase your desire to spend to the point where you reach saturation and give into a shopping binge? Are you rigid in your demands on your addiction, in that you tell yourself you will never shop again? As mentioned earlier, unrealistic demands can provoke a shopping binge—you become angry, lash out at the restrictions, and go overboard. What will help you is to customize a contract that realistically assesses your own situation and enables you to move through the many moods of recovery from a bad habit.

Developing a realistic contract with yourself is an excellent way to understand and stick to managing your habit. A contract is best shared with another trusted person—a counselor, friend, or group member whom you trust to give you constructive feedback and honest appraisal.

Your next step is to take the information you've gathered on your previous forms and develop strategies to protect yourself from these influencing events and behaviors. Be as specific as possible. Also know that you can revise or modify your strategies at any time.

Ask your trusted adviser to help you stick to your contract. Be specific about how that person can help you be diligent.

Evaluate your contract periodically, more frequently in the first year, and update it or change it as necessary.

Contract

Make copies of this form

1. When I experience the urge to shop, I will share my feelings with _____ as soon as possible.

2. I promise myself to follow these preventative steps on a daily basis and whenever I get the urge to shop.

    a. _____

    b. _____

    c. _____

3. I will cultivate these new, healthier behaviors to manage my shopping habit.

    a. _____

    b. _____

    c. _____

4. I will share the results of steps 2 and 3 with _____ by this date _____.

5. I will evaluate this contract at these times with_____ and make changes as necessary.

Evaluation dates: _____

_____

_____

Sample Contract

1. When I experience the urge to shop, I will share my feelings with _my counselor_ as soon as possible.

2. I promise myself to follow these preventative steps on a daily basis and whenever I get the urge to shop.

    a. *Allow myself to spend only $20 a month on myself.*
    b. *Write down my goals and keep them posted. I will read them daily.*
    c. *Give credit cards to my husband.*

3. I will cultivate these new, healthier behaviors to manage my shopping habit.

    a. *I will stick to an exercise program (swimming) three times per week.*
    b. *I will begin saving $100 per month.*
    c. *I will give myself positive affirmations daily for sticking to this contract.*

4. I will share the results of steps 2 and 3 with _my counselor_ by this date _in six months from today (2/14/93)._

5. I will evaluate this contract at these times with my counselor and make changes as necessary. Evaluation dates: _6/1/93, 8/1/93, 10/1/93, 12/1/93_

Some Closing Wisdom

The coming chapters will offer various techniques and alternatives to help you regain control of your shopping habit. It's worth taking a moment to pause now, to give yourself a pat on the back and some words of encouragement. The self-contract is one way to do that. But it can also help to think how much you know about recovery already. It can help, too, to hear some wisdom from those who've been down the path you're entering.

Many people have recovered from compulsive behavior. Compulsive shoppers, in particular, often return to normal spending habits with few traces of their earlier problems. Carol, for instance, shrugs and says she simply got "tired" of shopping—as if she'd been eating the same favorite food every day and finally couldn't taste it anymore, much less appreciate or enjoy it. She still shops, of course, but now generally with her husband (who has always watched his money carefully) and only when she needs specific items for specific occasions.

Now think about how much you have to teach yourself. Think of other habits you've stopped: perhaps you have stopped smoking or have changed your eating habits. Or simply think about one-time favorite pursuits that you outgrew or that no longer fit your lifestyle. Shopping can be that way for you. It takes an initial force of will to break through the habit, but once you're on the other side whole new vistas open up, and the desire to turn back disappears.

7

Anxiety and Stress Relief

Many compulsive shoppers find it hardest to resist the call to the mall when the pressure's on. Shopping can seem the perfect distraction from daily stress and anxiety. Shopping may be the *only* distraction that comes to mind. But, as you've no doubt learned, compulsive shopping just leads to more stress and anxiety down the line. When you realize that you've bought more than you meant to, or when the bill comes and you stash it away with a guilty feeling, knowing it will come back to haunt you, or when you worry that you're out of control, you simply add to the pressure you already feel. Out of habit, though, you may just seek relief by shopping more. It's a vicious cycle.

The good news is that you can break the stress and anxiety cycle. Stress is a physical, mental, and emotional response to various cues in your environment. Anxiety is one of the negative emotions that can accompany stress, the feeling that things are becoming out of control. While you can't always control cues from your environment, you can learn to control your responses to them. Your mind, as you'll soon learn, has astonishing control over the stress response of your body. A few learned skills can help you take the edge off that pressure—without resorting to shopping. Once the cycle is broken, you will no longer be at the mercy of a pounding heart, sweaty palms, and panic.

This chapter will teach you several tried-and-true relaxation techniques. Some, such as deep breathing, you can learn instantly. Others may take a bit of practice to use effectively. Ultimately, if you follow the steps in this chapter patiently, you will find yourself with an array of techniques to draw on anywhere, at any time stress and anxiety threaten to take hold.

A Few Words About Stress

When life throws trouble your way—or when a whole heap of troubles pile up and you feel close to breaking point—your mind and body react in predictable ways. First comes a physical reaction. In response to lightning-fast messages from your brain, your heart rate speeds up, your muscles tense, and you may begin to sweat; perhaps your mouth becomes dry, and your breathing grows rapid and shallow. These are the reactions that prepare you for "fight or flight." Once your brain has sent these prepare-for-danger messages throughout your body, it begins to process the situation consciously. You become aware of negative thoughts; you worry that you can't cope or that you need to escape; you may begin to panic. These physical and mental reactions feed into each other to keep the adrenaline coursing and your anxiety level high.

Stress is not necessarily a bad thing. Once upon a time that "fight or flight" reaction allowed humans to escape charging mastodons and stand up to club-wielding cavemen. Today, of course, stress reactions help you swerve away from oncoming cars or muster the energy to finish a task by deadline. Short-term stress can be productive and even lifesaving. But over the long term, ongoing stress puts tremendous demands on your body. A normal stress reaction gives way to relaxation, letting the body recoup its energies and rebuild its resources. When your stress is chronic—as when you indulge in a habit that only furthers stress—your body and mind suffer undue wear and tear.

Of course, you know that you don't like to experience ongoing stress. That may be precisely the reason you turn to shopping: it offers that short-term relief your body so badly needs. But there are far more effective blocks to stress—alternatives that don't cost a dime or come back to haunt you at the end of the month.

The trick to overcoming stress is to block the reaction at its early stages, before it has time to create mental turmoil and build on itself. Once you've recognized the physical "alarm" signs, you can take active steps to redirect the energy produced by stress. You can block the negative messages your brain puts out, misinforming you that you can't cope. And you can begin to calm your body. The anxiety won't have a chance to reach panic level. What's more, you'll approach the situation from an outlook of control, not fear.

This week, make a point of paying attention to your body. Everybody's stress reaction is different. What happens to you when you realize you'll be late for work? Does your heart pound, or your mouth become dry? What are you aware of first? More to the point, what happens to you physically when you feel "driven" to shop? These are questions you began to explore in chapter 5: your physical cues to shop. Once you can identify them, you can begin to use positive stress-fighting techniques.

Anxiety and Habit

Anxiety is one stress symptom that deserves special attention. One theory of habit formation suggests that anxiety is the primary driver of habit. A sufferer from any habit—drinking, nail biting, shopping, compulsive sexuality—has learned that the habit is an effective reliever of tension. It's a conditioned response: I feel anxious, I engage in the habit, I feel better (for the short term). After relying on the habit for a while, it can begin to seem the *only* relief for tension. When the habit is not available, the tension increases inordinately and begins to seem unmanageable. The panicked feeling is that I can't *stand* avoiding shopping. I cannot function without it; I am not strong enough to make it without it; I will be horribly deprived if I cannot buy something.

These beliefs are irrational. In every case, the feeling of panic fades with time even without turning to the habit. But most addicted spenders (or drinkers or nail biters) don't give the feeling enough time to go away by itself. They return to their habit before learning that the feeling will dissipate, given time.

It is only short-term thinking, of course, that makes the habit seem so appealing and necessary. Once you emerge from the short-term crisis, you wonder what you're doing with a car full of clothes you can't afford. You wonder how you'll pay the bill at the end of the month. This process leads to more anxiety down the line—and eventually more habit indulgence. If you take the time to slow the process down, however, the long-term reality will set in *before* you shop.

Most of the relaxation techniques in this chapter can help you defuse that moment of panic. The physical techniques will help you calm your body down—and buy you enough time for the irrational thoughts to subside by themselves. But you can also choose to counter those thoughts rationally. This is the basis of the first anxiety-fighting technique.

Technique One: Refuting Irrational Ideas

Chances are you spend a good deal of time talking to yourself. Don't worry—it's not a sign of craziness. Most people keep in close touch with their feelings, emotions, and progress in the world through a constant stream of "self-talk." Unfortunately, much of that self-talk can be negative. (It's been said that people say things to themselves that they would never permit themselves to say to their friends—or to their pets.) Have you ever told yourself, "I'm such an idiot! How could I have said such a thing? He probably thinks I'm a complete dolt now"? If so, those statements were probably followed by a plunge in your self-esteem, confidence, and mood. The things people say to themselves are their real interpretations of events and—whether or not they are based in reality—have real physical and emotional consequences.

It can be hard to spot your self-talk, since many of the messages you send yourself are near-instantaneous. Some messages become so conditioned and familiar that you hardly "hear" them before you respond. You see a thin model and think "I'll never be that attractive weight, I'm such a fat lug." But the thought itself isn't perceived—just the sight of the thinner woman and the "instant" emotion of feeling blue. The shorthand works so fast that you might even think that the emotion comes first, and then the words. Psychologists and researchers have spent plenty of time analyzing this process, and you can benefit from their finding that the self-talk almost always comes first.

The trick to overcoming self-talk is to hold yourself to reality. When you're in the midst of a shopping crisis, you may tell yourself anything from "I have absolutely nothing presentable to wear" to "I will die if I have to remain cooped up in this house and cannot go to the mall." You know rationally that neither of these statements is true. You have been going out and about dressed perfectly fine for your entire life. No one ever died from not being able to go to the mall—or even from having to stay in the house all day. Once you can hear your self-talk, you can refute it. That's what you're going to do.

There are five steps to this technique. Begin as soon as you feel shopping panic come on.

Step 1. Write down the facts.

What happened? What did you see? What did you do? These are the "shopping cues" you read about in chapter 5.

Step 2. Write down your self-talk.

Put those negative thoughts into words: spell out the beliefs, accusations, fears, or assumptions that pop into your head.

Step 3. Focus on your emotions.

How would you describe your emotional reaction in one or two words? Write them down. (Refer back to the list of feeling words at the end of chapter 5 if you need some help identifying your emotions.)

Step 4. Dispute your negative self-talk and irrational ideas one at a time.

To do this, ask yourself:

a. What does my common sense tell me about this statement?

b. What concrete evidence do I have to support it?

c. Is there any evidence against it?

d. Would a trusted friend or loved one believe this statement? How would he or she correct it?

Step 5. Substitute alternative self-talk.

For each negative statement, write down a rational comeback. Rely on the reasoning in step 4.

Here is what one man sat down and wrote before letting himself rush off to a record store.

Step 1. The facts.

I just heard a new CD on the radio. It's the newest album by a group that's wildly popular now. I want to play it for Cindy when she comes over tonight.

Step 2. What am I saying to myself?

I've got to get this album. Cindy will be really impressed, think I'm up-to-date with the music world and cool. If I don't get it, she'll know how out of it I am—I don't have anything else to play. I really have lousy taste.

Step 3. What is my emotional reaction?

Anxiety. Shame. Fear.

Step 4. How true are these statements?

a. Common sense. *Well, she probably won't like me or hate me based on the music I play.*

b. Concrete evidence for. *I have no idea what Cindy's taste in music is. I also don't know whether she likes this band or not, or even whether she cares what music other people listen to. No, I have no evidence that the album will make a difference to her.*

c. **Evidence against.** *She already likes me enough to come to dinner, so she must trust my skills and tastes to some degree.*

d. **What would my best friend say?** *Bob would roll his eyes and laugh. He loves the old records anyway. He'd probably say to play what I like and not worry about it—either she'll like it or not, and what difference does that really make?*

Step 5. Rational comebacks.

Negative Thought	Rational Comeback
I've got to get this album.	*I am not compelled to get this album. I don't NEED it, like air or food. I've lived perfectly well without it up to now! Also, I'm saving my budgeted splurge this week for that new book.*
If I don't get it, she'll know how out of it I am.	*Cindy will know little or nothing about me based on the music I DON'T play. Anyway, who says I'm out of it?*
I don't have anything else to play.	*I have plenty of records I love. (Not to mention the records I bought to please other people.) I can play what I like and reveal something about myself.*
I really have lousy taste.	*I know myself and what I like. Who is to say objectively that it's good or bad taste? Plus music isn't the only thing in the world to know about.*

Chances are you can come up with rational comebacks for any negative thought you present to yourself. The real trick is getting those irrational thoughts into writing. Once you see them on the page, they lose some of their power to terrify you.

Some other rational comebacks might be:

More Rational Comebacks

Negative Thought	Rational Comeback
I cannot function without shopping.	*I have survived most of my waking hours in life without shopping.*
Shopping is one of the few pleasures in life; I deserve that reward. (Poor me.)	*Yes, I deserve a reward...but one that really IS a reward. I'll benefit more from a long soak in a bubble bath. That way I'll still feel great tonight.*
If I can't buy myself something new, I won't go to that party.	*Of course I can go out with old clothes! All the clothes I own are things I once loved. They look new to others. Anyway, how I carry myself is what people notice and appreciate. And I am not dependent on their approval.*
I need to keep up with the latest styles and my friends. I need to see people at the mall. Without that, I'm going to feel alone and lost.	*The mall is not the world. (I can go for a walk to the park to see people and enjoy the day.) And I create my own style—I am not a fashion sheep!*
I'm so bored and lonely and depressed. Shopping makes me feel better, faster.	*I only think shopping will make me feel better, faster. In a few hours, it will make me feel much worse.*

Make copies of the blank form on the following 2 pages. Fill one out any time you feel a sudden plummet in emotions that might lead you to turn to a short-term solution you don't really like. If you allow ten to twenty minutes to really think the process through, you'll find that your panic has subsided during the time you spent in thought.

Refuting Irrational Ideas

Step 1. The facts.

_____

_____

_____

Step 2. What am I saying to myself?

_____

_____

_____

Step 3. What is my emotional reaction?

_____

_____

_____

Step 4. How true are these statements?
a. What does my common sense tell me?

_____

_____

b. What concrete evidence do I have to support it?

_____

_____

c. Is there any evidence against it?

_____

_____

d. What would my best friend say?

_____

_____

Step 5. Rational Comeback:

Negative Thought   *Rational Comeback*

_____	_____
_____	_____
_____	_____
_____	_____
_____	_____
_____	_____
_____	_____
_____	_____

Whatever you can do to slow down your habitual response will work in your favor. Resist the feeling that you must shop: that's a sign that you're locked in short-term, habit-driven thinking. Fighting against your irrational thinking is one powerful counterforce to shopping. Any one of the relaxation exercises below can also fill your time productively and calm you down.

Technique Two: Deep Breathing

This stress-breaking technique is so easy and accessible that you may not quite believe the power it has to calm your body and mind in any kind of trouble. Breathing is one of the first physical systems to change during stress, becoming rapid and shallow. That change is not always helpful, since large quantities of oxygen keep your body primed and tense. By learning to regulate your breathing and slowing down the rushed intake of oxygen, you can stop the stress reaction from building and bring peace and calm to your entire body.

Before you learn to take deep breathing to the streets, try the simple exercise below to familiarize yourself with the process and benefits of deep breathing.

On-the-Floor Deep Breathing

1. Lie down flat on your back on a carpeted floor or a towel. Uncross your legs, and allow your arms to rest comfortably at your sides. Close your eyes.

2. Turn your attention to your breathing. Place one hand on your chest and one on your stomach. Take a deep breath and notice how each hand moves as you inhale and as you exhale.

3. Now you're going to exert a bit more control. Keep the one hand on your chest and the other on your stomach just above your beltline. Begin to breathe in slowly and deeply. Let your breathing make the hand on your stomach move up as much as possible, while the hand on your chest moves up just slightly. Let the hand on your stomach rise higher than the hand on your chest, as you push the air deep within you. Hold for a moment, feeling the fresh, clean oxygen fill you up.

4. Now begin to exhale slowly, feeling the hand on your stomach move down first, followed by the hand on your chest. Blow all the air out of your lungs in a stream through your mouth, feeling all respiratory waste fly out of your body. Let your stomach collapse in, moving your diaphragm up to expel every last drop of air.

5. Did the "natural" breathing in step 2 feel different from the deep, measured breathing of steps 3 and 4? Think for a moment about the differences. The measured, fuller breathing of steps 3 and 4 is the way you want to breathe to relax and refresh yourself.

6. Enjoy several more slow, deep breaths with your hands still on your chest and on your stomach. Continue to breathe regularly so that your stomach moves all the way up while your chest moves slightly. Hold for a moment and then let your stomach move all the way down, along with your chest. Breathe slowly and deeply, feeling the soothing oxygen flow in under your control and all tension and worry fly out as you exhale.

7. Focus on the rhythm of your breath as your chest and your stomach move in a smooth flow. Try to release the tension through-

out your body, so you almost melt into the floor. Count five full, deep breaths and then relax.

On-the-floor deep breathing can be helpful any time you feel worried or anxious at home, whenever headache or other bodily pain flares up, or when you just want to relax. Insomniacs have long benefitted from the tranquilizing effects of deep breathing—especially when their thoughts begin to run wild at 4 a.m. It's true, however, that you can't always stretch out on the floor when anxiety strikes. Not to worry. The deep breathing exercise below is one you can use during a traffic jam, on a bus, or anytime you fear that you're losing control over your thoughts or your shopping habit. Stop your thoughts from running wild, and follow these simple steps:

One-and-Two Deep Breathing

1. Straighten your posture, so that your lungs have plenty of room to expand. Keep your spine straight and your bottom tucked under (don't arch your back) and make sure your shoulders are hanging as loose and low as possible. Keep your head level.

2. Begin inhaling and expanding your stomach, and feel the fresh air fill you all the way down. Concentrate on counting, saying "one" to yourself.

3. Continue inhaling and hold for a moment. Say "and" to yourself when you feel full enough to burst.

4. Begin to exhale slowly, letting all tension fly out with the used air. Feel your stomach move back in. Say "relax" to yourself as all the air leaves your system.

5. Inhale slowly and deeply again, counting "two" this time. Say "and" when you've taken in all the air you can and "relax" as you slowly exhale.

6. Continue focusing on breathing and counting, as you move through "three and relax," "four and relax," "five and relax," etc., all the way up to "ten and relax." Keep your breaths deep and regular. Push all thoughts out of your mind except for the

process of breathing and counting. By the time you reach ten, a new lightness and calm will have taken hold.

7. Relax your posture, and picture all the cells in your body bene-fitting from fresh, red, oxygenated blood coursing through your veins. Your body and your mind are relaxed and under control. As you return to normal breathing, remember to keep your pos-ture straight and your breathing smooth and regular.

Option: Deep Breathing and Visualization

If you like, you can combine deep breathing with visualiza-tion. A visualization is any mental image you can create and focus on—it's a little bit like deliberate daydreaming. By finding a con-crete, believable image for your troubles, you will have an easier time controlling the effect they have on you. What's more, you can contrive creative ways to get rid of them.

As you prepare to visualize, create as calm and peaceful a state for yourself as possible. Try to find a quiet place. Settle into a deep, comfortable chair if you can, and close your eyes. You might find it helpful to take ten good, deep breaths before you begin.

Below are a few visualization ideas that might appeal to you. As you read them, other ideas may come to you. Take a moment to jot them down.

- See each separate worry as a balloon of a different color. With each breath out, you blow one up—and let it float away. (Blow it up as you exhale and see it float away as you inhale for the next balloon.) Feel your load get lighter as you watch each balloon float far into the distance, out of your sight and mind.

  (*A blue balloon says I'm unattractive. There it goes into the sky! My fears about my looks don't matter at all now. Green must be envy. All those women with "perfect" lives and figures! Away they float—I couldn't care less. Red is money trouble. It floats into the sky, leaving me calm and peaceful and whole.*)

- Picture yourself in a peaceful, lovely place. Perhaps you're in the countryside by the banks of a fresh, flowing river. As you breathe in, feel the clean mountain air rush in. Blow your city trouble away with each breath out. Hear birds sing, imagine the sun shining down on you, and savor a mini-vacation as you relax far from your worries and fears.

- At the same river scene, make a little paper boat of each of your troubles. Watch them rush away as you send each one down the river, around the river bend and out of your line of vision. You're left alone with your peace and quiet.

Technique Three: Cue-Controlled Relaxation

This powerful relaxation technique is actually a combination of several widely used relaxation techniques. Blended together in this way, these techniques can allow you to relax thoroughly in less than a minute. That's quite an advantage over the twenty minutes required by most relaxation techniques. Of course, you'll want to allow yourself some time to work up to this point and savor each of the steps along the way. Each technique can be helpful to you individually when you have more time at your disposal.

Cue-controlled relaxation was developed by a physician named L. G. Ost in the late 1980s. It is designed to be used in any stressful situation you encounter throughout the day—making it a perfect antidote to the flood of triggers you may feel urging you to shop or to the surge of panic you experience in the middle of a mall. While the early stages of cue-controlled relaxation involve tensing and releasing various muscle groups, later stages help you relax without any tensing. You can put this powerful technique to use wherever you like and no one will notice.

You will experience the benefits of deep relaxation after just a few sessions. But remember, this is a progressive program. Each new stage of the program will help you relax more quickly and more deeply, until you can relax at will in about two minutes. Be sure not to rush yourself. You want to master each step of the program before you move on to the next step. Allow yourself one to two weeks, with a couple of practice sessions a day, to master each step. If this seems like a lot of effort, bear in mind that you're likely to find practicing one of the most refreshing points of your day.

At various points in this technique, you may find it helpful to create a cassette tape as a guide. (Prerecorded tapes are also available through New Harbinger Publications, if you prefer.) The specific directions below can be transferred easily to tape. If you do choose to make a tape, it will free you to put the book down and concentrate all your energy on relaxation. That can be quite a treat.

Stage One: Progressive Relaxation

Large muscles in your body bear the brunt of tension and stress. Without even realizing it, you may walk around with a clamped jaw, hunched shoulders, and an unnecessarily tight back. This tension takes its toll on your health, balance, and overall feeling of well-being. Progressive relaxation works by isolating the various large muscle groups and systematically detensing them. Focusing on one group at a time, you first tense and then release the muscles where tension builds. You begin to feel the enormous difference between tension and relaxation in these muscles, which will help you consciously relax each one when you need to. In addition, you will experience a much deeper relaxation in all your muscles after deliberately tensing them.

Your first session of progressive relaxation will focus on two main muscle groups: (1) your hands and arms and (2) your head, neck, and shoulders.

Begin by finding a comfortable chair. Rest your arms at your side and let your legs fall slightly apart. Settle down into the chair until you feel easy and relaxed.

1. Close your eyes. Take a deep, deep breath into your stomach and hold it in. Release it slowly, feeling your chest and your stomach become relaxed and loose. Relax your entire body as much as possible as you exhale.

2. Now turn your attention to your right hand. Clench your fist tight, studying the tension as you hold it. Feel the tension begin to creep up into your forearm as you continue to squeeze that

fist. Notice the strain. Feel your hand and forearm begin to burn and quiver.

3. Release the tension, feeling the muscles go limp. Your right hand is relaxed, and your fist begins to open. Feel how heavy and warm your hand and forearm are. Notice the difference between the strain of tension and the ease of relaxation. Your hand may feel warm, heavy, tingly, or all three. Notice how much heavier and warmer it is than your left hand and arm.

4. Be sure not to hold your breath during this exercise. Let your breathing remain calm and regular as you tense and as you relax.

5. Turn your attention to your left hand and arm. Follow the same procedure—tensing, and then relaxing—on the left side. Concentrate on the difference between tensing and relaxing. Notice how relaxed and heavy and warm your whole left arm becomes.

6. Now clench both your fists. Hold for about five seconds and feel the tension burning.

7. Release. Notice the feelings of warmth and heaviness and relaxation. See how these feelings deepen after repeating the tensing and releasing twice.

8. Now clench both fists and lift them, bending your elbows and flexing your biceps. Study the tension in both arms from your fists, up through your forearms and into your biceps. Try to make your arms quiver with tension.

9. Release. Let your arms fall back gently to your sides, completely relaxed.

   Next you will turn your attention to your head, neck, and shoulders. These are the muscles in your body most likely to lock in stress.

1. Take a deep, soothing breath. Hold it for a moment and release slowly.

2. Turn your attention to your head. Raise your eyebrows as high as you can, wrinkling your whole forehead. Hold them up and feel the tension on the top of your face and head.

3. Release. Smooth out your forehead. Imagine your entire forehead and scalp becoming as smooth as silk and at rest.

4. Close your eyes now and squint them tightly together. Hold them shut tight and feel the tension.

5. Release. Let your eyes remain gently and comfortably closed. Enjoy your smooth, relaxed face. Note the difference between tension and relaxation around your eyes.

6. Clench your jaw now. Bite hard enough to feel tension, but not so hard that you hurt your teeth. Notice the tension travel throughout your powerful jaw. Hold it tight...and release. Let your lips fall slightly apart and feel the relaxation spreading. Note the contrast between tension and relaxation in your jaw.

7. Now press your tongue against the roof of your mouth. Force it upwards and feel the ache in the back of your mouth. Hold it...and release. Allow your mouth to fall slightly open again. Relax as the warm, calm feeling takes over.

8. Press your lips outward now into an O or a kiss. Really stretch them out, pressing them together and feeling the strain. Hold it...and release. Let your lips return to normal. As you relax, notice if your lips feel tingly or warm.

9. Notice how your forehead, scalp, eyes, jaw, tongue, and lips are all relaxed. Make sure your breathing is calm, deep, and regular.

10. Move your head back as far as it can comfortably go and observe the tension in your neck. Roll your head to the right and feel the changing location of the tension. Roll it back up and to the left. Straighten your head and bring it forward, pressing your chin against your chest. Feel the strain in your throat and the back of your neck.

11. Release, allowing your head to return to a comfortable position. Let the relaxation deepen and notice how much tension has melted away from your head, chin, neck, and throat.

12. Now shrug your shoulders. Keep the tension tight as you hunch your head down between your shoulders. Hold it tight...and release. Allow your shoulders to drop back down. Feel the relaxation spreading down from your head and face to your neck, throat, and shoulders. Your shoulders are hanging limp, loose, and heavy.

Spend several days going over the first two parts of this exercise. It's best to practice twice a day—perhaps once in the morning and once in the late afternoon or evening after tension has had a chance to creep back in. When you feel comfortable with the technique and note a marked difference between tension and relaxation in the muscles of your hands, arms, face, head, neck, and shoulders, move on to the next major muscle groups: (3) your chest, stomach, and lower back, and (4) your legs and feet.

(NOTE: If you have a back injury, it may be wise to go easy on section 3 or to skip it. Consult your doctor if you have any concerns.)

Each of the steps below moves a muscle group once. You may find it helpful to repeat each step twice to deepen the relaxation effect. Once again, you may also choose to record a tape of the steps below. If you do so, keep your voice smooth and regular, allowing about five seconds for each tensing and ten seconds for each release. Remember, there's no need to rush through relaxation.

1. Begin by settling into a comfortable chair in a quiet location. Close your eyes, take a deep breath, and relax.

2. Move your attention down to your chest as you take another deep, deep breath. Inhale until your lungs are completely filled, pushing your stomach out. Notice the tension in your stomach and chest. Hold it...and exhale, releasing the tension slowly. Let the air blow out of your mouth in a smooth stream. Breathe normally as you continue to relax, letting your breath come freely and gently for the next thirty seconds. Feel the calm and peace spread through your chest and body.

3. Now suck your stomach muscles all the way in and hold them in. Really tense those muscles, making your stomach as concave as you can. Hold it...and release. Let your stomach fill out to a natural and comfortable position. Notice the difference be-

tween this easy, relaxed feeling and the way your stomach felt when it was tense. Your chest and your stomach are loose and comfortable now, holding no more tension than they need to do their work. Your breathing is smooth and natural.

4. Without straining, arch your back. Concentrate on the tension you create in your lower back. Feel the muscles pull around the middle. Hold it tight...and release. See how it eases your whole body to relax your back. Just let the relaxation sink into your body, deeper and deeper.

5. Notice the calm throughout your chest, stomach, and back. Remember how it felt when these muscles were straining with tension and savor the easy, loose, heavy feel of complete relaxation in the middle of your body.

You're now ready to move your attention down to the large, powerful muscles in your legs. Remain seated in your comfortable chair and take another deep, cleansing breath. Your eyes are still closed and relaxed.

1. Tighten your buttocks and thighs by pressing your heels into the floor as hard as you can. Squeeze those muscles. Focus on the tension, until it starts to burn or tingle. Hold it...and release. Feel your body settle back down, becoming looser and looser. Think about the contrast between the tensed muscles and the relaxed muscles in your buttocks and thighs. Let the lower half of your body feel heavy and warm.

2. Now curl your toes slowly downward, making your feet and your calves tense. Don't strain so hard that your feet cramp, but hold the tension. Hold it...and release. Let the relaxation flood your calf muscles and spread down through your feet to your toes. Notice how relaxed your calves and your toes feel.

3. Flex your toes up toward your face, putting strain on your shins and the bottoms of your feet. Hold those toes up and feel the tension. Hold it...and release. Allow your shins to relax deeply as your toes settle back down. Are your toes tingly or warm? Notice the difference between the tension and the relaxation in your shins and feet.

4. Sit still and feel a heaviness throughout your body. Let the relaxation deepen. Relax your feet, ankles, calves, shins, knees,
   thighs, and buttocks. Let the relaxation spread to your stomach,
   lower back, and chest. Take a deep breath and feel the relaxation
   move to your shoulders, arms, and fingertips. Remember the
   tension, but let it all go. Notice the feeling of looseness in your
   neck, jaws, and all your facial muscles. You have replaced all
   the tension with a feeling of deep relaxation.

That completes stage one of cue-controlled relaxation. Allow
at least a week to feel comfortable with the entire process of progressive relaxation. When you get up after each session, your body
should feel looser and more at ease than it did before you sat
down. Perhaps your mind will feel lighter as well, as your thoughts
turn away from daily worries and toward the comfort and health
of your body. Enjoy working through these exercises. The positive
benefits of the exercise should stay with you for several hours after
each session. Before you move on to the next stage, be sure you
feel comfortable with all the steps of progressive relaxation—and
have noticed a consistent relaxation benefit.

Stage Two: Release-Only Relaxation

Once you've felt the contrast between tensing and relaxing
each muscle group, you're ready to move on to "release-only" relaxation. This stage will cut the amount of time you need to relax
in half. As you probably guessed from the title, the idea is to relax
each muscle without having to tense it first.

Sit in a comfortable chair with your arms at your sides. Move
around a little until you are comfortable. Close your eyes and relax.

1. Breathe into your stomach...and out. Continue to breathe in full,
   calm, even breaths. Feel the relaxation deepen with each breath.

2. Relax your forehead, smoothing out all the lines. Keep breathing
   deeply and relax your eyebrows. Just let all the tension melt
   away, all the way down to your jaw. Your lips separate, and
   you relax your tongue. Keep breathing and relax your throat.
   Notice how peaceful and loose your entire face feels now.

3. Roll your head gently and feel your neck relax. Release your shoulders, letting them drop all the way down. Let the relaxation travel down through your arms to your fingertips. Your arms are heavy and loose. Your lips are still separated, because your jaw is relaxed, too.

4. Breathe in deeply. Feel your stomach expand. Now breathe out slowly in a smooth stream through your mouth.

5. Let the feeling of relaxation spread to your stomach. Feel all the muscles in your abdomen release their tension. Release your waist...and your back...and continue to breathe deeply. Notice how loose and heavy the upper half of your body feels.

6. Turn your attention now to the lower half of your body. Feel your buttocks sink into the chair. Relax your thighs... and your knees. Feel the relaxation travel through your calves, to your ankles, to the bottoms of your feet...all the way to the tips of your toes. With each breath, feel the relaxation spread.

7. Now scan your body for tension as you continue to breathe. Your legs are relaxed. Your back is relaxed. Your shoulders and arms are relaxed. Your face is relaxed. There is only a feeling of peace and warmth and relaxation.

8. If any muscle felt hard to relax, turn your attention to it now. Is it your back? Your thighs? Your jaw? Tune in to that muscle and tense it. Feel the tension and hold it tighter. Squeeze...and release. Feel it join the rest of your body in a deep, deep relaxation.

As with the separate stages of progressive relaxation, give yourself some time to master the release-only stage. The directions may seem simpler, but the tasks involved are a bit more complex. Be certain that you are draining all the tension out of each muscle you turn your attention to. Don't let the tension creep back in as you turn your attention to different muscles. When you stand up after a session of release-only, you should feel as relaxed if not more so than you did during progressive relaxation.

On the other hand, you don't want to make yourself crazy with strict directions. If you can, *allow* your body to relax, rather than forcing it to. If you have trouble with a particular step, take a deep breath and try it again—or skip it. If negative thoughts crowd your mind ("I can't even do this right!" "I *must* relax now"), try simply to notice these thoughts and let them go. Allow them to pass in and out of your mind, as you observe without judgment and concentrate on your breathing. Otherwise, they only create anxiety and become stumbling blocks to relaxation. If you passively observe negative thoughts flowing away, they will eventually cease altogether.

One or two weeks is not too long to devote to this stage of cue-controlled relaxation. Practice twice a day, if you can. Begin to enjoy the lasting benefits of deep relaxation breaks throughout your day.

Stage Three: Cue-Controlled Relaxation

Finally, the main stage of the game! Cue-controlled relaxation reduces the time you need to relax even further: down to two or three minutes, in most cases. In this stage, you will focus on your breathing and condition yourself to relax exactly when you tell yourself to. Be sure you are comfortable with release-only relaxation before you begin.

Make yourself comfortable in your chair, with your arms at your sides and your feet on the ground. Close your eyes and settle in.

1. Take a deep breath, hold it, and release slowly through your mouth. Now begin to relax yourself, from your forehead all the way down to your toes, using the release-only technique you've been practicing. See if you can relax yourself completely in thirty seconds. If you need more time, that's fine, too. (If you're making a tape, pause for half a minute to allow time to relax.)

2. You feel peaceful and at ease now. Your stomach and your chest are moving in and out with slow, even breaths. With each breath, the feeling of relaxation deepens.

3. Continue to breathe deeply and regularly, saying "breathe in" to yourself as you inhale and "relax" as you exhale. (If you're

making a tape, read these words into the tape, allowing about six seconds for each repetition.)

> Breathe in...relax.
> Breathe in...relax.
> Breathe in...relax.
> Breathe in...relax.
> Breathe in...relax.

Feel each breath bring peace and calm in and send worry and tension out.

4. Continue to breathe this way for several minutes now, saying the words "breathe in" and "relax" to yourself as you breathe. (Do not record the words again on a tape—this section is best done by saying the words to yourself, in silence.) Focus all your attention on the words in your head and the process of breathing. Let your muscles settle into deeper and deeper relaxation with each breath. Let thoughts of peace and relaxation crowd out the worries that would love to come in and take over.

Practice cue-controlled relaxation twice a day, as with the earlier stages. After each session, you may want to make note of the time it took you to relax and also how deeply relaxed you became. You may also want to try taking this technique out into the world with you. Try to calm yourself in a traffic jam or during a difficult day at work. Remember to begin by relaxing through release-only and then turn your attention to your breathing and the words "breathe in" and "relax."

Taking It to the Mall—or Not

Once you feel up to it, cue-controlled relaxation is the perfect tool to bring with you into the wild world of shopping. Many compulsive shoppers report feeling overwhelmed once they step into a store environment. No matter how strong their resolve to restrain their shopping, all their worries, fears, and deep dark shopping urges seem to rain down upon them once they step through those swinging glass doors. Cue-controlled relaxation gives you a measure of control over these forces. You can sit right down on any bench or stoop and relax completely. Once your body and your mind are relaxed, you'll be more in control of all your desires and actions. What's more, taking a break between impulse and action is the primary means of breaking down a habit-conditioned response.

Ideally, you want to relax your mind and body at the earliest signs of trouble. If you're sitting at home musing over an upcoming event and your thoughts turn to worry, stop and take notice. This may be just the thought process that typically gives way to an urge to buy a new outfit as a "pick-me-up" or a confidence-booster. If you can recognize that the urge comes out of the stress you feel around the event, you can redirect your energy towards calming yourself down. Take a relaxation break *before* you get to the store. Once you're calm and in control, you'll be in a far better position to reevaluate your desire to shop.

The ability to take relaxation breaks can serve as a valuable time-wedge to fend off that sense of urgency to buy something and also as a mini-vacation in itself. Shopping often seems the ideal escape from whatever trouble or stress your daily schedule offers. If you realize that you can relax and refresh yourself completely without even opening your wallet, you will feel a new sense of control and a new range of options.

Technique Four: Take a Hike (or a Swim or a Dance Class)

Next time you feel stressed, why not try going for a walk? Just pound the tension out on the pavement and let the neighborhood flowers and trees work their sensual magic on you. Get lost if you can. Bring a Walkman if you like. Or, for a more complete escape from your everyday world, go swimming. Go ice-skating. Sign up for that belly-dancing class you've been thinking about half-seriously.

Physical exercise is one of the most potent means of distracting your body with pleasurable, productive activity and generating a feeling of all-over well-being. It's a tried-and-true relaxation technique that works from the moment you lift a hand (or a foot) and keeps getting better. Whatever your level of physical condition, you can benefit from some form of regular exercise.

You'll enjoy it while you're doing it, if you pick the right exercise for your body; you'll sleep better at night; and your whole body will benefit from the devoted attention.

The most effective form of exercise is regular aerobic exercise. Aerobic exercise is any activity—walking, running, dancing, swimming—that gets your heart rate up to a particular training level, and keeps it there for twenty to thirty minutes. For a positive conditioning effect on your heart and lungs, you'll want to reach this level of activity at least three times a week. To figure out your optimal training level, a range of two different pulse rates, follow this simple formula:

1. Subtract your age from 220.

2. Multiply that figure by .65 to find the lower end of your training range.

3. Multiply that figure by .85 to find the higher end of your training range.

For example, if you are 25 years old, then your minimum conditioning heart rate is 127 (220–25, multiplied by .65) and your maximum conditioning heart rate is 166 (220–25, multiplied by .85). For a 35-year-old, the minimum is 120 and the maximum is 157; for a 45-year-old, the minimum is 114 and the maximum is 149. So if you are 35 years old, you would aim to keep your pulse rate between 120 and 157 beats per minute for about 25 minutes, three times a week, for optimum aerobic conditioning.

Begin any exercise session gently to let your muscles, including your heart, warm up. After about ten minutes of warm-up, move up to your training level for about twenty minutes. Then allow yourself another five to ten minutes of gentler movement as a cool down. Finish your exercise session with your favorite stretching exercises. This helps muscles stretch, seals in the beneficial effects of the exercise session, and allows your body to return gently to normal level. That's all there is to it.

Exercise is one of those things that can be extremely difficult to begin. Many people associate regular exercise with routine torture and suffering. This does not have to be the case—at all. Part of the trick to enjoying exercise is finding the activity that's right for you and your body. For some people running is the ticket to heaven; others prefer the gentler pace and ambling opportunities of walking around the neighborhood. If you're only able to achieve aerobic bliss while Top 40 music is blasting (even if you'd never admit you liked the stuff), then aerobic classes are for you; if you've always wanted to attain the grace of a ballerina, then dance class may be the way for you to go. Explore your options! There are plenty of exercise books out there and more classes in your local community than you can imagine. (Ever thought of learning karate? There are dozens of types of martial arts alone.) It takes a leap of faith and some willpower to get started. Just begin and give it a fair chance, and you'll find it even harder to stop.

A Final Technique: Learn To Do Nothing

Allow yourself to relax, for a change. Not much credence is given to inactivity in this culture. In fact, it can be hard to slow down. But learning to free your mind and your body from constant activity can be liberating.

Meditation is one means of achieving a calm, peaceful, do-nothing state. Yoga can also help you relax your body and your mind. You might want to explore the many instructional aids for meditation and yoga at a local library, bookstore, or adult education center. Or simply give yourself permission to take it easy for a while. Kick your feet up, take a deep breath, and try to find your own center of balance. You *deserve* a break!

8

Alternatives to Shopping: From A to Z

When you're a compulsive shopper, it can be tough to think of things to do other than shop. This is especially true when you use shopping as a way to reward yourself after a bad day or a big fight with your spouse. The mind gets stuck in tunnel vision and you play a trick on yourself by refusing to consider any other way to blow off steam or console yourself.

By reading this far you have already heard a good deal about the fallacy of using this kind of thinking—that going in search of more "things" to salve the wounds in your life only works in the very short run. In the long run you are still left with unsatisfied feelings, anxiety, a depleted bank account, and a whole lot of stuff you probably don't need.

On the other hand, you may actually deserve a huge reward. No matter what your relationship to shopping is or becomes, the need for some kind of reward in your life is a real need—and one that will only grow stronger when economic, family, and work pressures increase. Remember, there is no sense in depriving yourself of all pleasure. But your perception of what pleasure is needs to be redefined. You need to convince yourself that certain activities can and will give you as much pleasure as shopping—without the guilt or anxiety. You can give yourself rewards that have little or nothing to do with the exchange of money. That way your rewards are recession (and depression) proof!

The trick, of course, is to *choose an activity that you find rewarding*. Plan your day so that you make time for your special activity. One person had a bad habit of shopping right after work, which he gradually came to realize was a way to blow off steam. He didn't care much for exercise, so chose instead to start a flower and vegetable garden. In the summer after work he would attack the weeds with a vengeance, thus satisfying his need to expend extra energy. In the winter he would plan his garden and tend seeds in paper cups indoors. The following spring, he was amply rewarded. Instead of a bill to look forward to, he had riotous color and home grown meals.

The following suggestions are only a beginning. They'll help you get started by greasing the flow of your ideas and letting you open yourself up to the possibilities of all the things you can do in place of shopping. Some are activities that you can do on impulse, and others have the potential to turn into lifelong pursuits. While reading them, have a piece of paper handy and list any additional ideas that come to you. You'll want to include this list in your shopping journal for reference and to bolster yourself when you feel weak and about to give into temptation.

A

Arrange a garage sale. Get together with friends and neighbors. Fastidiously organize each section and mark up a price tag for each item. In other words, sell something (and let someone else do the shopping for a change).

Adopt a pet. Visit your local SPCA where there are usually dozens of lonely kittens, cats, dogs, and puppies yearning to go home. Take the time to brush your pet, research the right kind of food, and lavish them with your full attention. Cats aren't particularly walkable, but dogs are, and both can provide hours of distraction through petting and playing. Best of all, pets will reward you with unconditional love.

If dogs or cats don't appeal, investigate the possibilities of other kinds of pets, such as birds, fish, hamsters, ferrets, even snakes. A popular new pet making its way into many households is the potbelly pig, a miniature, completely housebroken, intelligent and loving little animal that won't shed or scratch the furniture.

B

Begin a book discussion group. Invite a circle of friends to read a book a month and discuss it over coffee and cake or wine and cheese.

Build something. Shelves, sculpture, a bird house...even a fancy layer cake. Your pride in making something on your own will add to the functional (or artistic) accomplishment.

C

Cook. Watch a TV cooking show. Drag out your old cookbooks and re-create favorite recipes; look through current newspapers and magazines for recipes that appeal. Learn the intricacies of a foreign dish. Invite people over to sample your efforts. (If you're a food binger or struggling with weight control, try out the other ideas listed here first.)

Clean. Clean your house. Clean out your garage or your attic. If cleaning in general seems too onerous a task, start small by cleaning a desk, filing cabinet, room, or closet. When you see the results of your efforts the next day, you'll be pleasantly surprised by the new order.

Compost. Begin a compost pile. Compost is easy to start, take care of, and keep clean, and it has very little odor. Dump all your kitchen scraps, garden clippings, and leaves in it and turn once a month or so. Avoid meat and cheese, since those attract animals, and twiggy sticks and vines which don't break down very well. You'll feel great when you notice less trash to take out each week, and you're doing your part for the environment—recycling your waste enriches garden soil.

Create. A story, a painting, a set of cards for an upcoming holiday. Let your artistic self shine through! If you catch yourself making self-deprecating statements like "I'm not artistic," banish the thought and try your hand at potato or apple prints (simply press a wedge of potato or apple on an ink pad). People love hand-made items.

D

Dad and mom. And family. Spend some time with them. Call them up. Invite them over.

Daily. Every day, take time for yourself. Relax. Meditate.

Devotions. Call on whatever higher or inner power for guidance and strength through devotions, prayer, or meditation.

Dance. Crank up the music and work up a sweat.

Donate. Donate extra clothes, toys, or canned goods to a worth-while local charity or shelter.

E

Explore. Explore areas in your town or city that interest you. Drive and look, or if it's safe, walk and look.

Editorialize. Remember that local—or national—issue you've been worried about? Voice your opinion through letters to the editor.

Emote. Go somewhere where you can emit an ear-piercing shriek. A great stress-reliever—really let 'er rip.

F

Form a clothes-swapping party. A woman in Virginia reports that one very successful way to satisfy the urge for "something new" is to invite friends over to swap clothes. About twice a year, ten friends or more gather in her house, bringing clothes they have grown tired of or outgrown, and a party ensues—mixing, matching, and swapping. It's great fun—you get to see your friends, share your opinions about what looks good or not, get rid of lots of clothes, and gain some new ones, all without spending a cent. One requirement: get a commitment from a volunteer before the party to take all unclaimed clothes to the local thrift shop or Salvation Army.

Fantasize endlessly of a vacation you are planning. Tell yourself that each dollar you save from not buying something goes into the kitty for your vacation. Watch your money grow. Make lists of how much you save by not shopping and what specific items you can buy while on your vacation.

G

Garden. Take up gardening: plant flowers or vegetables and care for them. When the time comes, pick them and arrange them attractively in a vase or deliciously in a salad. This can become a serious and all-natural habit. When anxiety strikes, zealously attack the garden weeds.

Go to the beach. Stretch out in the sand in the summer, or go ice-skating in the winter.

H

Hobby. Take up that hobby you've always dreamt about. Take a class: your local community college, YMCA or YWCA, or adult education center has plenty of ideas. Go to the library and take out books on knitting, model plane building, painting, dance...anything where the main idea is NOT collecting.

I

Image. Visualize yourself as strong, without needing to shop. Relax, create a mental image of all the circumstances that make your life satisfying and worthwhile, and allow yourself to feel fulfilled. Luxuriate in all the things you've created for yourself.

Index. Your recipes, coupons, addresses, special events, birthdays. You'll be grateful throughout the year.

J

Join an organization that you would like to be committed to. Join a local religious group, civic organization, professional society, or club. Think about community organizing. What needs to be done where you live?

Junk mail. Stop the flow of junk mail and catalogs into your mailbox. Remove your name from many direct-mail lists by writing to the Mail Preference Service, c/o Direct Marketing Association, P.O. Box 3861, New York, NY 10163-3861. Send letters requesting that other groups stop renting your name out. For more information about curtailing junk mail, contact Green Seal, P.O. Box R, Stanford University, Stanford, CA 94309.

K

Kite. Go fly one.

Knit. Knit, sew, cross-stitch, needle point. Create what you want for yourself and others from available material; avoid the temptation to buy more supplies.

L

Learn a foreign language. Brush up on (or begin to learn) a foreign language through classes or tapes. If you use cassette tapes, whenever the urge to shop strikes, you can drive around instead practicing your language.

M

Maintain what you own. It is amazing how many things lie around the house broken or torn, cluttering up the place. Think of the clothes that go unworn because they miss a single button. Right now, find two or more such items and fix them! Make a promise to yourself to continue to fix what you need and throw out what you don't.

Movies. Rent them. (Many local libraries rent videotapes for free!) Go to the theater. Invite a friend to join you. See a foreign film to practice your foreign language skills.

Music. Immerse yourself in music. Take up a musical instrument. If that's too ambitious, rediscover all your old records and tapes.

N

Neighbors. Do something nice for them.

Nostalgia. Get out those photographs stacked in bundles in boxes and drawers and organize them. Put them in albums. Label them. Throw out or give away those you don't need or want. Share your new album at the next family gathering.

O

Organize your closet. Make a list of everything in your closet. Take all things down from the shelves and organize them. Throw out what you haven't used. One person promises herself that if she hasn't used it or worn it in a year, out it goes. Redirect your compulsivity into having the cleanest, most organized closet you or your friends have ever known. Hang your clothes together in matching sets, so that you get a good feel for what you have.

Obsess about your money. Adopt a stance that your money is critical right now and needs to be carefully monitored. As soon as your cancelled checks come in each month, take time to reconcile your statement. Make a habit of knowing exactly how much money you have in your checkbook and in your wallet at all times. Be proud of that. Pay cash for everything. Pat yourself on the back once a day for doing all these things.

P

Put yourself on a shopping diet. Once you know exactly what's in your closet and on your shelves and which things are duplicates, plan your shopping excursions in detail. Promise yourself a *small* reward once a month, but no more than that. (If you can go longer, set an interval of two or three months between trips.) Give yourself a set amount that you can spend on these excursions (a manageable sum for your budget which you have discussed with your spouse, significant other, or buddy). Cut coupons, but only for those necessities you buy regularly, not frills. Go shopping with a specific mission, written down in your journal in advance, and don't stray from it.

Phone. Call up a friend or relative. Tell him or her what you're feeling. Find out what's going on with them.

Play. Take time for a game of cards or Scrabble or Trivial Pursuit or the newspaper's crossword puzzle. All can involve friends, and each can become an enjoyable habit.

Picnic. Get out that old blanket, invite a friend, be creative with leftovers, seek out a picnic location you haven't tried before.

Q

Quiet time. Whenever you feel that irresistible urge to get out there and buy, buy, buy, promise yourself a treat that you find truly delightful. Some people take soothing bubble baths full of their favorite fragrances. Some choose relaxation exercises.

R

Read. Go to the library. Hang out there, or take a book home—for free.

Restore old furniture. You know those old chairs, stools, and whatever you have stored in the basement? Now is the time to dig them out and fix them up, one by one. Take out a book on furniture restoration from the library and experiment. After you're done, you can bask in the satisfaction that you've brought something discarded back to life and saved yourself some money in the process.

Rearrange the furniture in a room. Nothing like it for a whole new feeling at home. (It's good exercise too.)

S

Solicit support from friends and family. One of the best ways to follow through on behavioral change is to make a commitment in front of friends and family. There is something magical about publicly announcing a change you desire—and publicly committing yourself to it. Find yourself a buddy or two and enlist their support. Be sure to let them know as much as possible about what you will need them to do for you. List your expectations and hopes. Make your list simple and uncomplicated so that you don't scare them off from the task! Tell them:

1. When you know your weakest times are
2. What you usually do in those cases
3. What you want to do differently (be specific)
4. How they can help you in that endeavor

For example, do you want them to take an active role in keeping you from your shopping behavior? Or would you prefer that your buddies simply listen to you as needed and provide a supportive ear? Make it clear beforehand how your buddy can help you.

Sex. Discover or rediscover the pleasures of lovemaking. Get into it. As they say, the best things in life....

Start. There's no time like the present for taking up that book or project you've always dreamt about.

T

Teach. Teach children something they want to learn. Offer to show adults how to do something you love to do. Teach something like flower arranging or cooking for a nominal free.

Take a bath. Take a bath or shower or jacuzzi or hot-tub break. Luxuriate in it. Pamper yourself with a bubble bath and a home manicure or pedicure.

Take pictures. Focus your camera on your family, your house, your community, clouds, birds, whatever.

U

Unclutter. Organize your house, your desk, or your garage.

Understudy. Volunteer for a local play.

Usher. Check your local movie house for openings. Free movies are an attractive fringe benefit.

V

Volunteer. There is a perpetual shortage of volunteers in just about every organization you can think of. And people are very grateful for any help you can give. Pick an organization that appeals to you. If you're an animal lover, the SPCA; a book lover, the library. Other options: the hospital, local womens' or homeless shelters, museums, hospices, a political campaign. Do something splendid that shows the strength of your heart, not your wallet.

Visit a museum or local tourist attraction. Relish beauty you can't buy—but skip the souvenir shop.

W

Wash your car. Vacuum it too; clean the insides of the windows. Enjoy the clarity of your efforts everytime you drive.

Write in your journal. When you feel the urge to shop, sit down and write all about it. Write about your feelings, your thoughts, and anything that comes to mind. Don't censor yourself. Give yourself permission to be free flowing on paper. This is your private time—resist the temptation to feel that you're writing for someone else.

Write letters to friends. How many times have you felt guilty about not writing someone? Here's your chance to feel good about being in touch with them and brightening their day.

Write letters to your congressional representative. Congresspeople are constantly claiming that they want to hear from their constituents. Now's the time to let them know what you think.

Work. Get a part-time job to fill your spare time. Make some money instead of spending it.

X

eXercise. Take up walking briskly. A walking regimen has been shown to be as beneficial as regular aerobics. Just remember not to join one of those "mall walking" groups, and check with your doctor before embarking on any new exercise program. Walking is a great way to reflect and think. Or, take up swimming, aerobics, or dancing. You might even consider joining a team sport. Whatever exercise you choose, there's nothing like it for relieving tension, toning your muscles, and generating an all-around sense of well-being.

Y

Yard. Clean up your own or someone else's.

Yoga. A great way to stretch and relax. Check your library for books or look for inexpensive classes in your area.

Yacht. Find economical ways to learn power boating or sailing. The National Coast Guard Auxiliary offers an excellent course in boating and it costs next to nothing!

Z

Zero. Do absolutely nothing—zilch. Let all tension and worry melt away. Allow yourself just to sit. You spend most of your time working, running, worrying, and moving. Why not give yourself a break?

9

Fighting Back

By now you realize that the strong urges you feel to shop come partly from you, and partly from the world around you. Awareness of the specific form these influences take is the first step towards recovery. Taking an active role against them is the second step.

Awareness

From the moment you picked up this book, you have been working on the first part of the equation: awareness. Through reflection and record keeping you have been developing insight into your own needs, desires, and vulnerabilities. This kind of self-awareness can help you see why certain sales pitches push your buttons. It can help you build yourself up at the points where you're most vulnerable. Most importantly, a clear-eyed sense of self points the way toward finding new resolutions for your problems—resolutions more effective and less painful than your current, costly coping strategies.

Knowing yourself is the critical first step. Knowing how you react to the world around you is an important next step. Chapter 3 suggested dozens of ways sales experts—in the course of doing their jobs—manipulate basic desires and fears to get your wallet out and the cash register singing. Have you noticed any sales techniques you hadn't recognized before? Making a game out of searching for new enticements and gimmicks and pressures to shop is one way of distancing yourself from the effect these techniques have—and something you can have some fun with as well.

One of the aims of this chapter is to further both senses of awareness, inner and outer. The emphasis will be on the effect of the outer world on your inner world, so that you can measure what you see against what you believe, what you want for yourself, and what you need. Sometimes sales gimmicks, catalogs, TV commercials, and magazines lead you to buy something you really do need. But more often, they try to sell you a product that has nothing to do with the desires they trigger in you: a craving for approval or love or youth. You want to recognize these techniques and build yourself a healthy cushion of skepticism. Your reward will be a new distance which will leave you far less vulnerable to ad-sells.

Keep in mind that in challenging the sales pitches, images, and even physical spaces that make up much of today's culture, you'll be going against the grain of society and peering into things you've long taken for granted. You'll also be shattering some illusions and comforts. Just remember that you'll find new comforts—healthier than your current habits. And since your current behavior and beliefs have led to some trouble, why not try something new?

Action

If the first aim of this chapter is furthering awareness, the second aim is to inspire you to actively resist sales pulls. Below you'll find game plans for watching TV ads, seeing through mail-order catalogs and magazine ads, and even surviving a trip to the mall. Don't just read about them here: try to implement as many of these techniques as possible. Watch TV with your checklist in front of you, looking for new types of ad-appeal. Walk through the mall with your notebook open, ready to spot new and "irresistible" sales techniques. Have some fun! But remember that challenging these familiar and powerful appeals is serious business.

This chapter calls for action combined with inner-awareness. Continue to monitor your feelings and reactions carefully, following the record keeping you began in chapter 5. Beware of sudden changes of heart and strong urges to give in to your desire to shop! Think of these moments as testimony to the strength of marketers' techniques—and remember that your own willpower is a stronger force. Look at not shopping as a game and be ready to include new observations and insights about your shopping behavior in this society.

As you work through each section, think about which advertising appeals have the greatest effect on you—either because you feel their power as you watch or listen or because you end up buying the products they tout. Have faith that you can resist even the strongest calls, and replace them with healthier behavior.

How To Watch TV

You may already think you're hardened to TV commercials. Perhaps you turn off the sound. Perhaps you chuckle at the ridiculous situations and claims the commercial announcers present. You may simply watch with half a mind, while the other (more rational) half reminds you that none of this stuff has to be true just because the announcer says it is. Still, however hardened you think you are to TV sales pitches, they can exert a hypnotic pull.

To really get behind the credibility and lure of advertisements, you'll want to break down each message or image you see into its sub-messages and sales techniques. The instant you see certain pitches, you want to recognize the hard sell behind it. Once you see what's really going on, you'll be aware of the potential for exploitation of your own needs and desires. Ideally, you'll be able to satisfy or acknowledge the need the sales pitch brings up without giving in and buying the product which probably has nothing to do with your needs, anyway.

All ads work around two feelings: envy and anxiety, as art critic John Berger has pointed out. To trigger envy, ads present someone in a position you'd like to be in—whether driving a lux-urious car, or acting eye-poppingly satisfied or looking young and sexy (flanked by members of the opposite sex). You envy the sub-ject of the ad, but more importantly, you envy an image of yourself that could be. The message of the ad is that the people have un-dergone some magical transformation that you could experience too, if only you would buy and use the product. Such ads awaken your great hopes for yourself and channel them into the desire for purchase. Ads that work around anxiety trigger the same feelings, but in a negative way. They arouse your fear that you will undergo the negative transformation suffered by the ad character—social isolation or disease and death—unless you buy and use the prod-uct. In each case, you get the feeling that only the product can save you.

To get around this, you need to focus on the logic behind the ad. Each ad, no matter how vague or indirect the situation or image, has a certain argument to it. Once you can state the argu-ment, you're well on your way to seeing why you respond the way you do, and why the ad is no answer.

Eleven Most Common Arguments of TV Ads

If you use this product...

1. You will join a wonderful group of people.

2. You will feel appreciated for all you do.

3. You will be rewarded for all you do.

4. You will be held in high esteem by others.

5. You will have more love or sexual gratification in your life.

6. You will enjoy the relaxation or adventure or escape you crave.

7. You will be more like certain famous or wealthy people.

8. You will be associated with success or humor or tradition or modernity.

9. You will find deep satisfaction.

If you do NOT use this product...

10. You will face social isolation or career failure.

11. You will be at higher risk for death or disease.

Each of these desires and fears is legitimate. The problem, of course, is that few have anything to do with the product the advertiser is touting. In order to remember this, it helps to follow the logic a few steps further. Take a look at argument 1, the claim that using a product will give you membership in a wonderful group of people. You've seen this argument countless times: think of the soft-drink commercial depicting scantily clad teenagers having a wonderful time around a mountain pool. The argument is: If I drink this soft-drink, then I will belong to this group of people. Belonging to the group might represent youth or carefree fun or playing with attractive members of the opposite sex. Each of those images can be a powerful pull. What the commercial will have you focus on is not the message—clearly ridiculous, logically—but on the feeling of wanting to belong. Your job is to focus back on the message.

First, state the argument clearly. *"If I drink this soda, then I will belong to this group of young models having fun in a mountain pool."* There are several messages in this argument. To identify which have the greatest pull on you, break them down into their smallest, clearest, logical parts.

If I drink this soda, then I will belong to a group.

If I drink this soda, then I will belong to a group of young people.

If I drink this soda, then I will have fun.

If I drink this soda, then I will escape to a mountain pool.

Be sure to consider every aspect of the commercial you may respond to. Look for all its possible messages to you, even those not explicitly stated. How do people look? How do they act? The people in the soda commercial are depicted as:

Young

Happy

In a group

Having fun

Relaxed

Maybe on vacation

Maybe not worried about money

Healthy, in good shape

If I drink this soda, then I will not be worried about money.

If I drink this soda, then I will feel like I'm on vacation.

One or more of these messages is bound to appeal to you. The question is, are any of these phrases true? Or even possible? Ask yourself what the link is between the product and the feeling. Ask whether the product has *anything* to do with the feeling. Chances are it won't take you long to arrive at a resounding NO! once you've identified the real argument.

Your goal is to remain rational about every ad you see. Don't let the ad convince you that the feeling it is selling is connected to the product. The feeling is one thing, and the product quite another. Indeed, the joy you might feel at a well-done commercial has everything to do with the commercial itself, or the possibilities that it raises, and little or nothing to do with the product. Try this game for yourself.

TV-Watching Game

Use the following list as a scorecard the next time you watch TV. Make several copies of it, so you can play the game as many times as you like. For each commercial that comes on, identify what type of ad you think you're watching and check a box next to the appropriate description. If the ad makes a particularly strong appeal to you, underline the description. Don't worry about right or wrong answers—it's your impression of the ad that counts.

Once you have identified a particular ad's appeal, state the argument of the ad as logically as you can. Then follow the logic through. Ask your questions out loud, if you like—if you can make yourself or people in the room laugh by recognizing the fallacies of an ad, you've got the right idea (and a new fun type of interactive TV watching). A few suggestions are offered after each ad type, along with a fill-in-the-blank format that you can use.

At the end of your TV-watching session, look over your responses. In thinking about which ads exerted the strongest pull on you, see which ads you noticed most often. Also think about any products you saw that you wanted for the product itself and notice what kind of appeal the advertiser used. Perhaps this will tell you something more about why the ad really appealed to you. Have some fun with this, but be honest, too. Your goal is a healthy distance from the seduction of ad-appeal.

☐ **This is an appeal to my need to belong.**

If I use this _____, then I will belong to this group of _____.

Is there really a link between belonging to this group and drinking this soda?

Do I want to be judged by the type of soda I drink (car I drive/ perfume I wear)?

Do I want to be a part of _____ because I use the right _____?

☐ **This is an appeal to my need to be appreciated.**

If I use this _____, then I will be appreciated by _____.

Is there a link between drinking this beer and feeling appreciated?

Does the beer company really appreciate me?

Does drinking their beer make other people appreciate me?

Would _____ help me feel more appreciated at _____?

☐ **This is an appeal to my need for reward for all I do.**

If I buy this _____, it will serve as my reward for

_____.

If I buy this gold bracelet, will I feel I've been rewarded for all my hard work? (Even when the bill comes?)

Does the jewelry company really want to reward me? (I'd be rewarding THEM with my money!)

Will _____ make me feel rewarded for _____?

☐ **This is an appeal to my need to be held in high esteem by others.**

If I buy _____, then _____ will think highly of me.

Do I really care what the car-parking attendant thinks of me?

Do I want to be respected by the shallow measure of the car I drive...even if it puts me in debt to have it? (How would I feel about myself then?)

Will buying ____ give me the kind of respect I want from _____?

☐ **This is an appeal to my desire for love, warmth, and security.**

If I use _____, then I will feel more loved/warm/secure.

Will stuffing instead of mashed potatoes make my family perfectly content and whole at the dinner table?

Will this appliance or vehicle provide my family with perfect love and security?

Is there a link between using this product and feeling love?

Will this _____ help me feel _____ ?

☐ **This is an appeal to my need for adventure or escape.**

If I use _____, there will be more adventure, escape, or relaxation in my life.

Will using that perfume make me adventurous?

Will drinking that soda be an escape?

Will buying that bubble bath give me any more time for relaxation?

Will _____ that _____ help me experience more adventure/escape/relaxation?

☐ **This is an appeal to my emulation of stars and wealthy people.**

If I use _____, then I will be _____ like
_____.

Will using the same shampoo as Cher make me a star?
(Is there a link between Cher's stardom and the shampoo she uses?)

Will using the same hammer as this TV handyman—an actor playing a handyman!—make me a better handyman?

(Is there a link between his skill as an actor-playing-a-handyman and the hammer he uses?)

Will using the same _____ as _____ make me
_____ like him/her? Is there a link between his/her
_____ and using _____?

☐ **This is an appeal to my fear of social isolation.**

If I don't use _____, then I will be shunned.

Is there a link between having friends and using this company's deodorant?

Would I want friends who judge me by the products I use?

Would _____ not _____ me because I don't
_____?

☐ **This is an appeal to my fear of death and disease.**

If I don't use _____, then I will become ill or die sooner.

Is there a link between death or disease and this product?

Is the "disease" one I've heard of before?

Is the "disease" one I've suffered from before? (Has a doctor confirmed this diagnosis?)

Is this problem serious enough to demand a cure?

Has a cure helped me in the past?

What would my doctor say?

Will using _____ cure me of _____?

Do I care about _____?

☐ **This is an appeal to my appreciation of humor or catchy music or sex.**

If I use _____, then there will be more humor, or music, or sex in my life.

Is there any link between eating these cookies and enjoying this music?

Will purchasing these products bring more humor or music or sexual gratification into my life?

Will using _____ make me share the qualities I admire in the ad?

☐ **This is an appeal to my _____.**

Is there a link between the product and the feeling?

Will using _____ really make me feel _____?

How To Read a Catalog

As you saw in chapter 3, catalogs portray very complete fantasy worlds. They portray people having the kind of fun you'd like to have and looking the way you'd like to look. It is tempting to step into this fantasy, and the catalog company does everything possible to make it easy to do so. You don't need cash to order, in most cases. You can speak to a personal assistant, who will tailor an order to your wish and ship it to you instantly (just like the care packages mom used to send to you at summer camp). All those pretty, happy models present themselves to you, beckoning. The seduction can be powerful.

As with television, you want to remain perfectly rational about the messages you're receiving. You want to think about all the cues feeding your impulse to pick up that phone and destroy your credit rating. The company gambles on the fact that it can sell you feelings and promises. Your job is to remember that they are really selling material goods just like the ones you already own. The feelings they promise can't be bought—for if they could, you'd be satisfied by looking over the contents of your closet.

As with television, catalog-reading can be fun once you know how to do it. The five steps below will get you started.

1. Don't Bother

Stop catalogs from coming to your home. Why tempt fate? (Can you imagine a recovering food addict subscribing to gourmet magazines?) Write to catalog companies and ask them to remove your name from the mailing list. A minute of pain can save a lifetime of debt. Don't worry—you'll find other things to read.

2. Analyze What You See

Chances are you won't avoid all catalogs. But from now on, you'll want to look at each catalog you see with a very critical eye. Be suspicious. Approach the catalog warily, determined to analyze each page and see what's behind each pitch that's out to trap you.

Think of the real world. Look at the models in their settings and imagine them walking around. Would a young woman in her bra and panties (and heavy makeup and jewelry) go wandering around a burned out building? Would the clothes fall as nicely if the models weren't in that exact pose? (Or the clothes weren't pinned behind them to fit perfectly?) Would the clothes look the same if the model were older? Larger? More stressed-out? Make yourself laugh as you imagine that young woman in a teeny skirt climbing onto her bicycle or showing up at work or looking twenty years older and a few pounds heavier in the same outfit.

Think of the real picture. Expand the window of the picture to include the whole setup: photographers, lights, wardrobe consultants, makeup artists. Think about how much these people cost! (And you know where that money comes from.) The same is true of the designers and printers hired to produce the catalog. The fantasy world that sails so easily into your mailbox is in fact an expensive investment made by the company to increase sales.

Think of the whole picture. What is the background out to suggest? Wealth? Vacation? Comfort? Chances are it's one or all of the three. Look at the symbols of wealth and fun. Now imagine these same people working or frowning or sick with colds. Remember, it's the image of vacation and luxury that the catalog is selling as much as it is the material items represented.

Throw out the messages. Just like luscious descriptions of menu items, transforming ordinary food into gourmet fantasy, little pitches can turn a hunk of plastic into Cinderella's glass slipper, ready to bring out the "inner princess" or the "true beauty" in you. "New!" promises change and novelty, as much in you as in your wardrobe. "Shades of Paris" or "Europe's newest shape!" promises mystery, passion, and tradition, banking on the fact that the foreign always sounds better than the familiar. Even little words like "Most popular item" give you a dose of peer pressure, suggesting that everyone else knows to buy these items. Remember, the catalog is selling clothes, not promises. Personal transformation takes more than a new blouse.

Look for the pressure. Note the ordering information ON EVERY PAGE. Clearly, they're ready to catch your first impulse. Note the promises of "personal service, available 24 hours a day."

Do they want you to feel appreciated by the salesforce, or guilty for leaving them idle? (And someone so nice, too! Someone waiting to listen to you and help you...even when your spouse or your therapist or your cat isn't.) Note the promise that overnight mail can let you wear tomorrow what you see today—as long as you call before noon. Just ask yourself some questions before you pick up that phone. Would you have gone naked tomorrow if you hadn't seen this ad just now? Would you still be interested if the same garment had been in back of your closet for six months? Or would you be looking for something else in these pages?

3. Analyze What It Costs

Give yourself a one-day time-wedge. You have plenty to think about before you're ready to order anything. *Eliminate the pressure by not allowing yourself to order anything the day you see it.* If it's an item you really need, the need and the catalog will be there tomorrow.

Add up the total. Don't get sucked into separating items: a T-shirt for $39, matching leggings for $20, coordinated belt for $35. Sure, each price may sound reasonable. But you're looking at a $94 total plus tax and shipping, at least another $10, or $104 all together. (Think about the actual material value of the outfit, which is probably far less than your total cost.)

Is more really less? Maybe that $39 T-shirt comes with a special offer of two for $60. Sure, you'd save $19 on the new T-shirt (telling you something about what the product is really worth). But you're also paying $21 more than you'd have to for the first shirt you wanted. Chances are you don't need a second one—you're only interested in it for the sale. You'd be paying $21 extra for the shirt you wanted.

Maybe the catalog offers a $20 rebate if you buy at least $150 (telling you something else about the cost of an item compared to its value). Well, then, you'll just add something else. Be aware that you're loading up your shopping cart...and your bill. Buying more to save money really makes no sense. You can't save money when it's already spent.

The bottom line. Imagine the total added to your monthly credit card bill...or deducted from your wallet right now. Think about how much of that money goes to fund the catalog and the models, and how little goes toward the material value of the clothes. Think about what other necessities you might buy with that money.

4. Analyze What You Want

Think about your material needs. One way to think about your material need is whether you'd be able to justify your purchase to a spouse or a parent (or your accountant). Do you believe your own explanation? Think about what it means to need something.

I need _____ because I do not have a similar _____.

I will use it when I _____.

True or false: I was looking for this item before I saw it here.

True or false: I do not have an adequate substitute item.

Think about your emotional needs. What feelings does a purchase promise you? Below are a few that might make sense. What others of your own can you add?

warmth	renewal	fun
connection	security	youth
sparkle	modernity	comfort
energy	polish	elegance
completion	reward	escape
pleasure	anticipation	excitement

Compare the feelings you have selected with your material need, above. Which do you think is the dominant factor in your decision to buy? If you suspect it might be the feeling, you now have a chance to find a cheaper way to get there.

Think about method of purchase. If you only want to place your order by telephone, ask yourself whether it is the purchase or the human contact you seek. If you can only imagine paying for your order with credit, ask yourself whether you could afford to pay cash as easily, or whether you are creating a fantasy you can't afford. Even if you're paying by credit card, take out your checkbook and deduct the cost. How does that feel? You're going to have to pay for it eventually anyway.

5. Get What You Really Want

Consider alternatives. If there is any way you think you can receive the rewards of purchase without resorting to shopping, chances are it isn't the item you really want. Based on your responses above, think about things you can do, see, or make that might satisfy your craving in a nonmaterial way. Go back to chapter 8 for some specific alternatives.

Consider your purchase. If, after a rational evaluation, you believe that you need and can afford the catalog item, send away for it. Remember, you're not out to deprive yourself of things you need. You just want to separate necessary purchases from impulsive, addictive purchases: things that you get to fill different needs. But also keep the next rule in mind.

Order by mail only. Don't allow yourself to order by phone. If you need the item tomorrow, you'll need it next week. It's important that you see the total and that you write out the amount rather than read numbers to a sympathetic voice over the phone. Slowing down your impulse to buy, as all the above steps require, will help ensure that you buy only reasonable and rational purchases. Generally, this means not ordering by catalog! And that means stopping them from coming to your house.

A Word on Magazines

Looking though a magazine can be as inspiring—and as depressing—as looking through a catalog. Magazine ads, of course, exert their own hard sell. These ads are more seductive than those on

TV or billboards, since they're tailored to your interests—whether high fashion, or stereo equipment, or electric guitar collecting. The glamour or sophistication you see is intended to spark your deepest sense of envy. (Not just for the model or the collector you see, but for a version of yourself that could be...if only you make the right purchases.)

In looking at magazine ads, keep all the tips for catalog shopping in mind, with particular attention to analyzing what you see. The environment you see in magazine ads is carefully assembled to suggest wealth or leisure or success—a complete look or feeling or lifestyle that you'd like to have. Try to deconstruct the messages in these ads as completely as possible, searching for both logic and emotional appeal.

It is important that you keep your guard up even when reading magazine articles. Remember that almost all magazines are sponsored by their advertisers. If magazines offend these advertisers, they go bankrupt. If magazines push their advertisers' products, they succeed. Treat all editorial suggestions as advertisements, not friendly objective recommendations.

Beware of pitches for "newness." Magazines depend on this quality as much as fashion designers do. If you did not need a new diet for each week, or a new makeup tip or guitar pick, you would buy one magazine and be satisfied. Of course, if this week's feature worked as well as promised, you wouldn't need one next week.

Realize that the orientation of every article in a magazine will support the views the magazine would like you to hold. An article telling you about the fun you could have at a clothes-switching party wouldn't run in most women's magazines, since the advertisers would protest the non-shopping solution. No hi-tech magazine will extol the virtues of a system released years ago while their advertisers are busy trying to move this season's hardware off the shelf.

Magazines can be fun. But that vague feeling of dissatisfaction that you often feel after reading one has the same source as ad-sell: you see yourself as inadequate next to the high-fashion models pictured or the talented actresses interviewed or the accomplished musicians reviewed. The magazine offers two solutions to this inadequacy you feel: (1) buy the products advertised and (2) buy the same magazine, next issue.

How To Deal with a Mall

Heading to the mall can put all your shopping-recovery plans to the test. You can put a magazine or a catalog down when you're tired. You can turn off the TV. But once you've arrived at the mall, you are engulfed in a sensory environment. The feelings can seem overwhelming—and leaving can seem as difficult as staying without buying everything in sight. For this reason, there are two alternative plans for dealing with a mall.

Plan A is for shoppers who have historically had trouble with malls. You know yourself—if you cannot enter a mall without losing sense of time and your bank balance, and if you must leave burdened with packages, you'll have to impose strict limits if you are to survive a mall. For Plan A shoppers, the best plan is often to avoid the mall. With a restricted shopping plan, however, you can emerge alive.

Plan B is for shoppers who feel some measure of control, but never trust that they won't go over their own limits. You may have popped in and out of the mall with no problem before. You may also have popped out feeling as if you've dropped all sense of reason. Plan B offers a model for reflective shopping, which will keep you in touch with your rational limits and your emotional triggers.

Steps one and two are the same for Plans A and B, and both are important. Think of the mall as a jungle you must cut through to get what you need. All the resistance skills you've been developing will come into play as you fight off the fierce native dangers: sales, gimmicks, and deals. You want to prepare the right tools and get through as quickly and safely as possible.

Step One: Preparation

A. Create a list. Write down only what you absolutely need from the mall. Are you certain you can only get these items at the mall? If there's another possibility, take it.

B. Create a budget. Write down the reasonable price range for the item you need. Write down how much money you can spend. Bring only that amount of cash with you, adding just enough extra for a lunch break, gas, and telephone use. DO NOT BRING YOUR CREDIT CARD. If it is a big budget item you need, such as an appliance, think of some place other than a mall to purchase it.

C. Go only when you're feeling strong. When you go to the supermarket hungry, you come back with too many groceries. When you go to the mall feeling vulnerable and unattractive (or empty and needy), you run the risk of running wild. Don't let such emotions drive your shopping expedition.

D. Bring company. Invite a friend who doesn't like to shop or ask your kids to come along. There's nothing like nagging to prevent lingering!

E. Make an escape plan. Plan a nice dinner. Make an appointment you'll enjoy keeping (a visit to the salon would be a better idea than a visit to the dentist, for instance). You'll be able to limit the amount of time you spend in the mall, and also make sure you have something pleasurable to look forward to.

F. Prepare coping statements. Look back through the exercises you completed in chapter 6. Remind yourself of the emotional needs that have triggered shopping responses and refute them now. Think about those parts of your life that you feel good about now, but that you tend to lose sight of when you shop. Review the other shopping experiences you've recorded. What coping statements would have helped you? Make your coping statements as specific as possible and address them to your particular needs and fears. Some examples:

> I know that my self-esteem suffers when I see all the things I can't afford.

> *I can feel good about myself as I learn to control my shopping urges.*
> *Every success helps me feel more powerful.*
> *I am worthy inside no matter what I wear outside.*
> *I accept and love myself as I am.*

> When I walk into the mall, my anxiety level skyrockets.

If I ring up an enormous bill, it won't make me any
less anxious.
I know ways to calm myself down.
I am anxious about my shopping habit, which I am
learning to control.

My journal says I feel like a failure if I leave the mall
empty-handed.

A full wallet is my sign of success.
Everything I DON'T buy is another victory against my
shopping habit.
If I want to accomplish something, I can paint the
shelves when I get home.

I don't get everything I deserve, so I might as well treat
myself well.

Overcoming my shopping habits is the biggest reward I
can give myself.
I deserve to feel great when the bill comes.
The best rewards aren't material.

Take this step seriously. Comb your old journal records—
and your memories—for thoughts that might trigger an urge to
buy. Refute those thoughts now, as powerfully and as specifically
as you can.

G. **Visualize a brief, successful trip to the mall.** Enjoy creating your own helpful daydream. Find a comfortable chair, settle
in, and close your eyes when you feel relaxed and peaceful. Let
every detail of your trip to the mall run before your eyes like a
film and see yourself emerge successful. Be sure to focus on sensory detail in order to make the dream real. Here is one example
of a visualization script.

I get into the car and drive past the bakery and the supermarket
and then all the car dealerships by the highway. I turn left into the mall
lot and park. My heels click as I walk across the pavement to the main
entrance. When I step into the mall, the quality of light changes. I hear
water running in the fountain and the murmur of shoppers strolling and
talking. The background music is just noticeable, regular and pleasant. I

can smell the coffee and cookies from the snack stop. There are sale signs at the leather shop and colorful promotions by the record store. I can hear the rock music beckoning from the record store.

I walk straight to the escalator and ride it up to the china store. Once on the next level I see other stores and promotions, but I feel happy and directed. Checking my list, I walk into the store and ask for the plate that matches my set. Other items look wonderful, but I remember that pitchers and serving trays are not on my list. I take the plate to the register and pay for it with cash. The saleswoman wraps it in crisp white paper and puts it in a silver bag, and I feel successful as I take it under my arm. She asks if I'm sure that's all, and I say yes.

Now I start to exit the store, but a display of big red crystal goblets catches my eye. I stop and walk over to them, feeling I just have to pick one up. My heart starts to pound. The goblet I pick up is heavy, and I admire the way the light sparkles and dances through it. I imagine creating an occasion to show them off to guests, and pouring amber after-dinner sherry into it...but then I STOP, and put the goblet down. My friends come over for my company, not my crystalware! If I don't buy it, I will save more than enough money for this week's entire grocery shopping. My heart is still pounding, but I walk out past the holiday displays by the register. I can feel that money still in my wallet, and it makes me proud.

I ride the escalator down, pass the record store again, and push open the big glass doors to exit the mall. The sunlight is blinding, and I feel the cold air hit my face. With the package under my arm I walk back to my car and savor the feeling of success. My hand remembers the weight of the goblet, but my brain announces it's proud that I didn't buy it. Even the sight of the shoe store from the parking lot can't break my feeling of control and victory. I drive home happy and with a feeling of control.

It's a good idea to visualize yourself feeling tempted and successfully resisting that temptation. Hold onto the feeling of leaving the store with only the purchases on your list and savor the feeling of success.

Step Two: When You Arrive

A. Be prepared. When you take your first few steps past those swinging glass doors, you may feel suddenly overwhelmed.

Everything that has made you shop compulsively may come flooding in. Don't give in to those feelings—or panic. You have the tools to understand the different messages and to combat them. You're more prepared than you realize.

B. Acknowledge your feelings. If possible, sit down by the fountain and write them down in your journal. Try to name as many feelings and fears as you can. What do you fear? What strength did you lose when you walked through those doors? What do you think a purchase would do to help?

C. Answer those feelings. Repeat the coping statements you prepared before you left home. If none hit the mark, create new ones that answer the anxieties and desires you're feeling. Recall the good things in your life and about yourself that have nothing to do with shopping. (Also remember what you've already decided: whatever you feel, the answer's not in shopping!)

I have nothing.

I have more material things than I can keep track of.
I am rich in health and in love.
I am strong and healthy, mentally and physically.
Overcoming my shopping habits is the biggest reward I can give myself.

D. Relax. Take a few deep breaths. Do any of the quick relaxation techniques from chapter 7. Especially effective is cue-controlled relaxation. Show yourself that you can take the edge off your anxiety without resorting to purchase.

At this point, Plan A shoppers who have historically had trouble with malls should skip to step five: Purchase and Depart. Plan B shoppers should continue through steps three and four.

Step Three: Beginning To Shop

A. Just looking. Resolve to walk around for the first half of your trip WITHOUT BUYING ANYTHING. Don't worry—you'll have a chance to get what you need. But the first half—watch your watch—will give you a chance to do some no-pressure, deep-reflection comparison shopping.

B. Keep track. When you see something you want, write it down. Even if you see something you HAVE TO HAVE, impose a time-wedge of at least half an hour. Don't worry, nothing you absolutely need will disappear.

C. Analyze the mall. Pretend you're a marketing scholar. How are you being manipulated? Are you being routed past too many stores? Is there a particular scent or image or sales ploy drawing you into a particular store? Does anything here make you angry? Alternatively, try to think of new ways to lure shoppers in. Write down things you see that might belong in a book about mall design. Or point out features you notice to your shopping companion.

D. Analyze yourself. Keep monitoring your feelings and notice how they change in the course of your shopping walk. Do any go away or change by themselves before you buy anything? If you talk to anyone, what role do you play in that conversation? Are you assuming the role of a flirter? Of a daughter? What cues are you following? All this information will be useful to you today and also good material to review before your next shopping trip.

Step Four: Half-Time Break

A. Rest. Buy a cup of coffee or sit by the fountain and stretch your legs. Now, as you sip, look over your notes. It's time to sort out what you want to do.

B. Reflect. Begin by checking your list. For each item you are considering purchasing, ask yourself:

Does the item appear on my list?
Is it within the budget I allowed?
If not, will I be able to justify it to my spouse or
partner? To myself?
Is there a concrete need this item will fill?
Does it make rational sense to buy it?

If you answered yes to all five questions go straight to step five. For any item you answered no to, fill in the questionnaire on the following pages. (You'll want to make several copies of it.) Chances are there are emotional or psychological reasons driving you to make that purchase. Your goal is to isolate the pull to buy.

The Why I Want It Questionnaire

*(**Make copies of this form**)*

1. Discomfort

Is there an uncomfortable feeling that purchase might make go away? (Will I disappoint a saleswoman? Feel ugly? Feel empty?)

What underlying feeling is it? (Anxiety? Loneliness? Sadness? Depression? Fear? Emptiness? Insecurity?)

How would the purchase fill or resolve it?

Does this make rational sense?

Will I really use the product?

Will the product continue to resolve the uncomfortable feeling?

Has purchase resolved this feeling for me before? (For how long?)

Do any of my coping statements refute this feeling? (If so, repeat them now! And take the hint that you've felt this way before.)

How else might discomfort go away without purchase?

2. Comfort

Is there a pleasant feeling I think the purchase would give me? (Will I feel healthier? Renewed? More attractive?)

What underlying feeling is that? (Comfort? Security? Attractiveness? Success? Joy? Relief? Belonging?)

Is there a rational link between this purchase and this feeling?

Do I own anything else that would give a similar feeling?

Will I really use this product differently?

Do any of my coping statements address this feeling? (If so, repeat them now!)

Is there anything I can do that will give a similar feeling?

3. Environment

Did I feel a need for this item before I saw it in the mall?

Did I like the setting I saw it in?

Did the salesperson influence my desire for this item?

Did I like the way the store made me feel?

Is this the feeling I am trying to create for myself with this purchase?

Are the feelings I want attached to the item itself?

Does it make rational sense to purchase it?

4. Cost and Reward

What is the financial cost of this purchase?

Can I afford it?

What will I have to give up in order to afford it?

What are other costs of this purchase? (Will it start an argument with my spouse? Make me feel out of control? Will I need matching items?)

What is the reward of this purchase?

Is the reward worth the cost?

Is there any way to get the reward without paying the cost?

The only way to score this questionnaire is to think about your responses and decide which seem the most important to you. In the process of answering the questions, you've had ample time to consider whether each purchase makes rational sense. Which category was the most meaningful to you? Which answers did you feel guilty about? Does the purchase still make rational sense?

Remember, deciding not to buy something is not depriving yourself of anything. It's rewarding yourself with new control, a more manageable end-of-the-month bill, and good feelings that will outlast the purchase.

Step Five: Purchase and Depart

A. Go to the stores on your list (and only those stores). Plan B shoppers may return to stores for any items they have justified in a Why I Want It Questionnaire.

B. Purchase the items on your list (and only those items). Plan B shoppers may add any items they have justified in a Why I Want It Questionnaire.

C. Pay in cash. (You did remember to leave your credit cards at home, right?)

D. Repeat your coping statements (as you leave the store and all the way back to the parking lot).

E. Congratulate yourself. However you fared, your exit is a triumph over all the forces conspiring to keep you in the mall and run your wallet ragged.

The Bottom Line

The effort to recognize and resist cues to shop is a never-ending game. For better or worse, you will continue to see new methods and ploys and gimmicks, and some of them are bound to entice you. Look for them. Listen carefully to all you hear. Then, when you've taken in all the colorful sights and sweet-sounding promises, *think*. Sales techniques may fool your eyes and your ears, but only momentarily. These sensory organs, easily seduced, have to report to your rational brain. That's where you can analyze the messages and make an intelligent decision about what you want to do.

In the course of working through this chapter, you will have felt the joys of an unravaged wallet. Perhaps you left the mall with enough money left over for your next trip to the grocery store.

Maybe you filed a catalog away and rearranged your living room. You might even have spent a pleasant hour at home, laughing at TV commercials and entertaining yourself for free. The bottom line is that you have discovered that you control your money and your responses. They do not control you.

The next chapter will give you a chance to apply this rational mastery to your own finances. As you may already have discovered, setting out with a budget takes the mystery and the fear out of money. You know what you can afford and what you can't. That doesn't mean there isn't room for impulse purchases and treats for yourself. It just means the treats you do allow will come without panic or punishment.

10

Taking Control of Your Finances

By Glenn Catalano,
Personal Financial Planner

In all probability, the motivation that brought you this far in this book is a sign that you are truly ready to begin taking action about your finances. Unfortunately, it's almost equally certain that you do not know how to begin. Few people do, and compulsive shopping is just one of many silly things that it's possible to do with money. So take heart—you're motivated, and change is possible.

There are several keys to controlling your finances. The very first one is to *stop your complaining*. Despite all the woeful stories that the media carry about the perils of living in a consumer economy, you are not a financial victim. You *are* the one who pulls the money out of your pocket, writes the check, or signs the credit card slip.

Contrary to popular beer and credit card commercials, you cannot "have it all" (unless you plan to file for bankruptcy every few years). What you can have is everything you need to make your life complete.

Think back over all the thousands of purchases you have made in the last ten years. How many of them simply led to more purchases? Did any of them ever give you a sense of completion? Few people look at money as a *tool,* something that can be used to manipulate and alter their environments. In fact, money has only one purpose, and that purpose is to provide you with options. If you have decided that your only option is to buy more CDs, shoes, earrings, or furniture, you have simply limited your life by your own lack of vision.

Let's start by laying down a principle, and the principle is: If on December 31 you still owe money for *anything* other than a home, a car, or the cost of education or health care, you have spent too much the preceding year. In fact, you have spent more than you've earned.

If you spend more than you earn in any year, you are financing your lifestyle with debt. Since you do not have the ability to print money or issue bonds, you cannot behave as the federal government behaves. If you are in debt at the end of the year, you are paying interest on your debt. That interest payment is money that you do not have to spend or save for your own goals.

Do you remember the last time you used your credit card to buy something that was on sale? It was a great deal and you couldn't resist it, but you didn't pay off your credit card at the end of the month. The interest you are paying on that purchase has negated the savings of the sale. Suppose you use your credit card to purchase a $60.00 pair of shoes for $39.99. Let's say you do not pay off that charge by the end of the month and continue to carry it throughout the year. By then, if your card has an interest payment of 18 percent, those shoes will actually end up costing you more than $47.00. (Eighteen percent is a median figure. Some cards charge as much as 21 percent, while others have recently fallen as low as 12.9 percent. If you must have a credit card, it pays to shop around for a low-interest one.) What's worse, after you've worn those shoes *once,* they're probably worth, at best, only $5.00 at your next yard sale. And people wonder why they can make no financial progress.

I have worked with people whose debt exceeded their monthly income. None of these people were pleased with their situation, and most wanted to do something about it. Those people who were committed to action were successful in changing their situation, as long as they did not start out by inventing excuses why they *couldn't*.

At the end of the chapter I will give you a four-step process to follow that will guide you in managing your money effectively. For now, here are nine tricks to attaining financial freeedom.

Trick 1. The first trick is one you play on yourself. People make the mistake of carrying their credit cards with them in case there is an "emergency." For years I've been hearing about these famous emergencies. But whenever I ask my clients to describe the last emergency when they've actually had to have a credit card, they can never remember a single one.

Trick 2. When you do go into a store to buy something, make sure you have a list of what it is you intend to purchase. If you do not have a list, leave your checkbook, cash, and credit card at home. Make your list as specific as possible.

Trick 3. The third trick is to avoid group shopping at all costs. Group shopping is when your family or friends call you up to ask you to go shopping with them as a recreational activity. The peer pressure in group shopping is enough to cause even the most resolute individual to buy impulsively. If you are a charter member of a full-fledged shopping team, it may be difficult for you to admit why you no longer want to join them at the mall. If your shopping buddies don't respect your attempts to change your behavior, this may be a sign that they too have some shopping problems to work out. Or perhaps you simply need new friends who are more attuned to your needs. (By the way, group shopping with children or with friends who hate to shop is a trick you may want to try.)

Trick 4. Everytime you make a credit card purchase, subtract the purchase from your checkbook. That way, there will always be money available at the end of the month to pay off the credit card bill. You will also be able to see how you deplete your available cash with each purchase. I started using this trick many years ago, and it works wonders for keeping track of where your money goes.

Trick 5. Cancel all of your credit cards *except* one major card. Simply cut each card in half and return it to the card company with a letter telling them you are cancelling the card. Don't worry: they will continue to send you monthly bills for your previous charges—but they won't send you a new card unless you request one. (An American Express card is a good choice for the card to keep, since all of the charges must be paid each month.)

Trick 6. Since these tips are not intended to be an exercise in self-deprivation, I advise you to set aside a specific amount of money at the beginning of each month to spend on yourself, with no limitation as to what you will buy with it. Do not exceed that sum of money, and do not use a credit card—pay by cash or check only.

Trick 7. If your checking account has overdraft protection, seriously consider eliminating this feature. I have seen many people succeed at getting rid of their credit cards and then fall back on this overdraft feature as a new source of expensive credit.

Trick 8. Those solicitations that come in the mail for new credit cards because you are a "valued" consumer should never be opened. Rip them in half and deposit them in the trash. In one year I saved all the credit card solicitations I received. Had I accepted all of them I would have been carrying 47 credit cards.

Trick 9. This is the final trick, and it's no trick at all. I have used this procedure with many people for years with outstanding results. Buy a small notepad, one that you can put into your pocket. Everytime you spend *any* money, whether cash or credit, take the notepad out and write down how much you spent and what you spent it for. If you spend 25 cents on a phone call or 30 cents for a pack of gum, write it down. If you buy a soda, write it down. At the end of each week, add up what you have spent.

This strategy doesn't come with a guarantee, but everyone who has used this technique has reported to me that they have immediately cut their discretionary expenditures in half.

What do I mean by *discretionary expenditures?* What we're really talking about here is discretionary *expenses,* which are best defined by comparison with their opposite number, necessary living expenses.

Necessary Living Expenses

Car payments

Food

Telephone and utility bills

School loan payments

Haircuts

Laundry and dry cleaning

Insurance payments

Mortgage or rent

Discretionary Expenditures

Gifts you buy for people

Another pair of shoes

Dining out

Movies

All entertainment and recreation

Most people have their greatest difficulty in controlling discretionary expenses. Simply put, they believe that most of these kinds of expenses are *needed.* In other words, they *must* have that dress or that new CD, or subscribe to that new magazine, or take that trip.

If you can control your discretionary spending, you will in all probability have discretionary *income* left over at the end of each month. Discretionary income is simply the money you haven't spent, which you can then allocate to saving or investments—or to getting yourself out of debt.

Figuring Your Net Cash Flow

Calculating your discretionary monthly income is not a complicated task. Taking it step by step, you simply add up your income
and subtract your expenses from it. The amount left over is your
discretionary monthly income.

Turn to the last page of this chapter and look at the form
labelled "Figuring Your Net Cash Flow." Part of effective money
management involves filling out a form such as this, which is simply a tool to help you understand where your money goes from
month to month. But note that it will only help if you fill it out
based on what has happened during the past month. If you complete it based on what you *wish* your cash flow would look like
or how you think it *should* look, then it will not be a realistic reflection of your present financial situation.

Notice that I am avoiding the word "budget." For most people, the term budget holds a negative connotation. You may auto-
matically think that it means suffering, deprivation, or limitation
of your lifestyle. Or you look at a sample budget sheet and think,
"This is too difficult to do." If you do find yourself making up a
thousand excuses for not figuring out your budget, you may be
thinking too negatively about what a budget can mean for you.
Try replacing the word "budget" with the concept "managing your
resources" or "financial plan."

In the end, much of the fear and panic that people feel about
their spending behavior comes from simply not knowing whether
they are spending available money or running up a deficit paid
for with borrowed, expensive money. Sticking with a money plan
will free you from this fear, since you'll know how much there is
and how much has to go where. Indeed, even if you "blow it" by
breaking a budget, a solid framework can put you right back in
shape by showing you how far to compensate to make up for it.
And remember, it's not what you earn or spend that counts—it's
what you get to keep for yourself.

Your Net Cash Flow Sheet will also be of great help to you
if you decide to see a financial planner. If you choose not to see a
planner, you can use the budget sheet as a catalyst for discussion
with your spouse about where your money goes.

Remember, we are calculating these figures on a monthly basis. The following steps will help you to complete this form.

Monthly Income

Wages, Salary, Tips. This number can be taken directly from your pay stub or, if you are self-employed, from your monthly operating statement. (If you are self-employed and do not understand what I am talking about, hire a bookkeeper or accountant immediately.) If your income varies greatly from month to month, whether because you are self-employed or receive bonuses, or any other reason, you can add up an entire year's income and divide by 12 to get your monthly average.

Dividends from stocks, mutual funds. If you receive monthly, quarterly, or yearly income from these sources, you need to average the dividends for the entire year (add them up and divide by 12). If you are unsure how much you receive each year, look up the amount you reported on last year's income tax form.

Interest on savings, CDs, bonds. If you have a savings account or an interest-bearing checking account or own CDs (Certificates of Deposit) or bonds, then you are receiving monthly interest income. Again, it will be necessary to add up the total of interest received during the year and divide by 12.

Capital gains. Capital gains result when you sell personal property and receive more money from the sale than you paid when you bought it. For example, if you bought stock for $100 and sold it for $200, your capital gain would be $100. Another example: that antique chest of drawers that you bought at the flea market for $10 and sold for $100 after you fixed it up.

Pensions, royalties. No matter what your age, you may be receiving pension income. The amount of pension income that you receive each month should be placed in this box. If you receive royalty income—for example, if you have written a piece of computer software or a book and you receive quarterly income from your publisher—you need to add up the four quarterly payments for the year and divide by 12 to determine the monthly amount.

Now add up the five previous boxes. This figure is your total monthly income.

Monthly Expenses

Mortgage payment or rent. Let's start with the basics. How much is your monthly mortgage payment or payment of rent to your landlord? Place that number in this box.

Vacation home mortgage. If you own a vacation home, place the amount of mortgage in this box.

Real estate taxes. You may or may not pay real estate taxes separately from your mortgage payment. If your real estate taxes are included in your mortgage payment, do not place them in this box.

Automobile loan. This is the amount that you pay to a lender for your car each month. If you are leasing an automobile and the lease is not a business expense, place the amount of the monthly lease in this box.

Personal loans. This is the money that you owe to individuals or banks for things that you have purchased other than an automobile or home. (Do not include monthly charge account payments.)

Charge accounts. This is the average monthly amount that you pay to credit card companies or stores. If you do not pay the same amount each month, take the average payment for the last six months. You should be able to find the numbers in your checkbook.

Income taxes. This is the amount you pay to your state and to the federal government. You can find this number on your pay stub. If you are paid twice a month, multiply this number by two to get the monthly tax that you pay. If you make quarterly payments to the government, divide the quarterly payment by three to get your monthly payment.

Social security. Again, this number can be found on your pay stub (marked FICA). If you are paid twice a month, multiply this number by two to determine the monthly amount.

Transportation. In this category, include your monthly expenses for operating your automobile or using public transportation. If you have a car, include the cost of all maintenance and repairs, fuel, tolls, and parking. Do not include the cost of your automobile loan or the cost of insuring your automobile. Take the yearly amount and divide by 12 to arrive at an average monthly expense.

Insurance. This category includes life insurance, disability insurance, automobile insurance, and homeowner's or renter's insurance. (If your homeowner's insurance is included in your mortgage payment, do not include it in this box.) If you pay your insurance in quarterly (or semiannual) installments, divide by three (or six) to calculate the monthly payment.

Savings and investments. Include money that you put away each and every month. If you are buying savings bonds through your place of employment, be sure to include the monthly amount in this category. If money is being placed into a retirement account for you by your employer, you will need to ask whether the money is pre- or post-tax. Include only post-tax contributions in this box.

Contributions. This is money that you contribute to charities, religious organizations, schools, or your favorite cause. If you give to a charity only once a year, divide that number by 12 to arrive at a monthly amount.

Household maintenance and repair. This is a difficult category. If you are living in an old home and constantly repairing or upgrading the house, estimate the yearly amount of your expenses and divide by 12. If you are living in a newer house, you can probably anticipate that any major work you have done will not be an ongoing expense. Accordingly, you can take the cost of recent work and make an adjustment to account for it—for example, by taking 10 percent of the repair and dividing that number by 12. Add this figure to your other ongoing maintenance and repair expenses and put it in this box. Be careful! If you have obtained a personal loan or put the repairs on your charge card and you have already counted the repairs or maintenance in the personal loan or charge account categories, do not count those expenses again here.

Furniture, decorating. Be careful in this category also. If you have used charge cards or personal loans to pay for decorating or furniture, do not count those expenses again if you have already included them elsewhere on this form. If you have recently purchased an expensive piece of furniture for cash and you rarely make purchases of this kind, divide that number by 12 to get an average monthly amount.

Gas. This category includes fuel oil, natural gas, or propane to heat your home.

Electricity. This is the monthly amount you pay to heat, cool, and light your home.

Telephone. This is the total amount you pay the phone company each month.

Water. This is the monthly (or quarterly amount divided by three) that you pay for water and possibly sewer connection.

Food. Do not include eating out in this category. This is the food that you purchase to prepare or consume at home.

Garbage. Do not include in this category your purchase of fast food. This category is confined to the fee you pay to have your trash removed from your home.

Clothing. This is the monthly amount that you spend on clothing for all family members throughout the year. If you have major expenses for clothing when the kids go back to school in the fall, divide this number by 12 and add it to the total. Do not count any clothing costs already included in the charge account category.

Medical. This includes all your nonreimbursed medical expenses. Don't forget the cost of all prescription drugs that your insurance company does not reimburse.

Entertainment and recreation. In this category include eating out, going to the movies, magazine purchases, book club dues, and vacations. This category can be difficult to track, especially if you go away for weekends or have expensive interests such as snow skiing or golf. Be sure to include the costs of your equipment.

Club dues. Include in this category all professional, fraternal, and social organizations that you pay dues to. Usually you pay these dues yearly, so divide the number by 12.

Education expenses. Include in this category tuition, books, room and board, and registration fees that you pay for your children or yourself to attend school.

Child care. Include here the cost of child care and babysitters.

Other expenses. Include in this box all veterinary bills, gifts that you buy for others, condominium association dues, and your children's allowances. If you spend a lot of money for Christmas gifts, divide this amount by 12 and include it here.

Add up all your monthly expenses to calculate a total.

Discretionary Monthly Income

Subtract your expenses from your income: this is the amount of income that you have left over at the end of the month.

Please note two things: first, your discretionary income may be a negative number. Don't despair—doing something about that negative cash flow is one of the reasons you're reading this book. The second thing to remember is that you can have a negative discretionary number and still not be in debt. You may be overwithholding on your taxes (as many people do). Once a year you get a large tax refund, and you use this money to finance many of your purchases. You are fooling yourself if you are doing this. The government likes you to overpay your taxes because they get to keep your money for a whole year without paying you any interest. Not a very good deal, considering many of the things they do with your money. It's in your own best interest to have the correct amount deducted by your employer.

Debt Consolidation

Let's look at the ways you can reduce the payments that you're presently making to the credit card companies.

First, you can consolidate your debt by going to a bank and showing them what you owe monthly on your credit cards. You may be able to qualify for a loan at a lower rate than you are presently paying to the credit card companies. The bank may or may not extend the credit to you, depending on your income and the amount of short-term debt you presently owe.

If you are substantially behind on your debt payments, another alternative is to go to your local consumer credit counseling agency and ask for help negotiating with your creditors. You may be able to work out a payment plan that gives you room to breathe and time to get your debts back to a manageable size.

Your last resort is bankruptcy. Bankruptcy is not a recommended solution, since it will taint your credit record for many years and may limit your possibilities for buying a home or a new car. Keep in mind, too, that filing for bankruptcy is really just a further extension of the same habits that you started reading this book to overcome. In any case, you would be wise to consult a financial planner before considering bankruptcy protection.

Financial Planning

Financial planning is not a mysterious process. It is no more than taking stock of where you are today and understanding where you need and want to be in the future. A competent financial planner can help you examine your present financial situation in depth and provide you with a set of recommendations based on your unique set of circumstances.

In general, a financial plan is based on a detailed analysis of your financial goals and objectives. Where do you want to be financially in the next ten or twenty years? When do you want to retire? Do you plan to provide for your children's education? Questions like these are reviewed in the context of your current financial status, including both your assets and your liabilities.

The financial planner will analyze the information you give him or her and present a written financial plan to you that identifies methods for achieving your goals and objectives. From there, you and the planner go on to take action based on the plan. For

example, you may establish a savings program to meet certain objectives.

Finally, you and your planner will meet periodically to review your progress and make sure that you are staying on track
to meet your goals. It is important that your financial planner make
a long-term commitment to your financial goals and that you feel
comfortable discussing your money and your attitudes about
money with him or her. Don't hesitate to tell a prospective planner
what you expect of your financial relationship. And remember that
a reliable financial planning professional will concentrate first on
identifying your needs, rather than on promoting products or investments.

A Four-Step Process for Effective Money Management

At the beginning of this chapter I promised a four-step process to manage your money effectively. By following these simple
steps, you will develop the motivation and self-discipline necessary
to bring yourself out of the debt cycle. As a result, you'll find your
self-confidence growing, and a power over your money that you
probably hadn't dreamed possible.

1. Reduce your discretionary spending by 5 percent and
   save that money every month. Write yourself a check—to
   your savings account or a specially designated account—
   at the beginning of every month. Treat this check as another bill—you are simply paying yourself first.

2. Keep your purchases on a strict cash basis. If the cash isn't
   available, don't make the purchase. This strategy works
   particularly well after you have become accustomed to
   paying yourself 5 percent at the beginning of every
   month. Really work at making pay-as-you-go a habit in
   your life.

3. Relish managing your money well. You're becoming one
   of the ones who plan and move forward, while others
   about you sink, mired in debt. Look forward to balancing
   your checkbook each month and take pride in knowing

the exact amount in your account. Hear the confidence in your voice when you say that you'll be out of debt by a specific date.

4. Don't let feelings of hopelessness cripple your ability to make changes. Whenever those hopeless feelings creep into your thinking, refer to the section in chapter 7 on refuting negative self-talk. Remind yourself that goal setting and money management are helping you move away from being a victim to having active control over your life.

Figuring Your Net Cash Flow

Monthly Income

Wages, Salary, Tips	$	Furniture, Decorating	$
Dividends from Stocks, Mutual Funds, etc.	$	Gas	$
Interest in Savings Accounts, CDs, Bonds, etc.	$	Electricity	$
		Telephone	$
Capital Gains	$	Water	$
Other Pensions, Royalties, etc.	$	Food	$
Total Monthly Income	$	Garbage	$

Monthly Expenses

		Clothing	$
Mortgage Payment or Rent	$	Medical	$
Vacation Home Mortgage	$	Entertainment & Recreation	$
Real Estate Taxes	$	Club Dues	$
Automobile Loan	$	Education Expenses	$
Personal Loans	$	Child Care	$
Charge Accounts	$	Other Expenses	$
Income Taxes	$	**Total Monthly Expenses**	$
Social Security	$		

Net Cash Flow

Total Monthly Income	$
Total Monthly Expenses	$

Transportation	$	
Insurance	$	
Savings & Investments	$	
Contributions	$	
Household Maintenance & Repair	$	

Discretionary Monthly Income   **$**

(Subtract your expenses from your income)

11

When the Going Gets Tough

So now what? You've read this book to the end and started to put the exercises recommended here into practice. You've admitted your problem and taken honest stock of your situation. You've kept a journal, talked regularly with your trusted friend or counselor, and found alternative rewards and stuck to them. Perhaps you've experienced success here and there—periods where you're able to stick to your shopping diet, where you feel you have some control. But then the dreaded day comes, and you lapse back into your old behavior. As if expending pent-up energy, you binge shop. You feel guilty. You blame someone or something else. You feel more guilty. You wonder if you'll ever change and you begin to despair. Your situation is hopeless. You are hopeless.

Perhaps you wonder why it is that you can wholeheartedly agree with the suggestions written in this book, but still succumb to the next sale. You shake your head knowingly at others' stories of shopping sprees and mounting debt, but you still find yourself right where you started—or so it feels. For many addicts, there seem to be two selves—one self who recognizes what must be done and another self who can't or won't take action on it.

These two selves can feel as if they are at war with each other. (Do you ever get the sensation that you are just standing by, watching your other selves battle it out?) You feel out of control, and you don't know if you have the courage to choose.

The step of adopting change into your life and making it stick is often the last great hurdle to any effort at change. People get stuck here—at the point of finally stopping smoking or giving up chocolate, they feel fearful of making the change permanent. They choose to stick with misery, rather than venture out into the unknown. Even though the possibility of greater happiness lies there, they fear the risk of greater pain. In effect, they fear change itself.

Everyone fears change to some degree. But when your current situation has become clearly worse than the alternatives—alternatives that you can imagine and that you know you desire—then fear becomes a roadblock to positive action. The anxiety perpetuates itself, instead of spurring you on to a new freedom and joy. What can you do to overcome this stalemate? This chapter is designed to offer a helpful little nudge.

Below you'll find ideas to renew your discovery plans while still leaving room for normal fear, a bit of backsliding, and some of the other perils that we humans bring on ourselves. This chapter draws on ideas presented throughout this book and knowledge that you've gained about yourself in the course of reading and thinking. In addition, a few spiritual guidelines are offered for you to keep in mind as you go through the frightening, exhilarating, courageous steps of enacting change in your life.

Get Specific: Nail Down Your Alternatives

You know from chapter 8 that there are plenty of things to do other than shop. No doubt some looked more interesting to you than others. If you can manage to cultivate a few options as attractive new habits, these activities will serve as preemptive strikes and block out the urge to shop before it interferes. It is essential that you narrow such plans down from "I guess I could organize a garage sale someday" to "Two weeks from Saturday would be a great time for a garage sale. I'll call the newspaper right now so the advertisement can get in by Thursday's deadline." Don't just tell yourself "Well, yeah, I've been meaning to take up dancing again," really do it: "I wonder if there's a drop-in beginners class today. I'll call a few places." The trick, of course, is to select activities that you truly enjoy.

Long-Term Alternatives

In the contract you wrote to yourself in chapter 6, you included favorite alternative behaviors. Remember these now. Have you taken action on any of them? If not, take a moment to pick your three favorite ones. Be specific about what you'll do and when you'll do it.

Three non-shopping activities I will include in my calendar this month (on these specific dates):

1. _____

2. _____

3. _____

If you've somehow talked yourself into picking activities that make you *groan* when you think about them, choose others. There's no sense in defeating your purpose before you get started by choosing something you would really rather resist. Besides, choosing something that you really do look forward to will give you that extra energy you need to get over the hurdle of inaction.

Tailored Alternatives

Learn to anticipate danger times—before a big party, for instance, or when you know you'll have to drive past a favorite store with time to kill. Earlier that week, plan *specifically* what you will do instead of shop. Perhaps a dance workout or a long walk and a bubble bath would lift your mood (and improve your body) before the party. Perhaps you can take an alternative route to your destination that won't take you past your favorite store—a route that might show you a bit of scenery or give you time to think on the road. Or you might go to a museum or outdoor concert that same day. You get the idea; now really think about upcoming problem moments that you can take care of now:

Upcoming danger spot:_____

I'm worried I'll _____

Why shop? _____

Instead, I'll _____

_____

Advance planning needed:_____

Example:

Upcoming danger spot: *Presentation to board of directors.*

I'm worried I'll *spend a fortune on a new dress.*

Why shop? *To increase my confidence. I'll feel "lucky."*

Instead, I'll *ask Dan to listen to a rehearsal report on Thursday and give me feedback (and praise). Take Rover for long walk before work on Friday.*

Advance planning needed: *Check with Dan (and Rover!)*

Emergency Alternatives

Ideally the more you plan in advance, the fewer crises you'll find yourself in. Still, the urge to return to old habits can be swift and strong. That's why you've got to have an emergency plan.

A good emergency plan gives you something you can do at the drop of a hat—something that you *enjoy* doing and that you can do nearly anywhere. Some particularly effective plans:

Call a trusted friend or counselor. Arrange this plan in advance so that your friend will anticipate such calls. Try to explain what you will need in these moments. Generally a sympathetic ear is more powerful help than a lecture or a litany of advice. (You know you shouldn't shop, but it's best if you hear yourself say it.) Relay these thoughts to your friends now. Try to enlist at least three different people who are willing to take on this role.

Engage in any physical activity. Go for a walk or drop in on an exercise group or dance class. Physical activity engages your body and your mind and provides an effective outlet for stress and frustration. It also leaves you relaxed and refreshed.

Do a relaxation technique. Deep breathing, cue-controlled relaxation, and visualization can all help you out of a fix and soothe your jittery nerves. Simply closing your eyes, breathing deeply, and focusing on a few favorite affirmations can restore your strength and will. Or you might focus on an image: see the urge to shop as a huge ocean wave that will pass, if only you can ride it out. Turn back to chapter 7 for more specific relaxation programs.

Study your journal. Turn to a section where you've recorded the negative consequences and emotions that follow binges. Imagine them now—either the money subtracted from your wallet, or the need to hide purchases from your spouse, or whatever you had a hard time with. Trust the wisdom your earlier self is imparting to you now.

When You "Blow It"

Despite the best of plans and intentions, relapses happen. Once you've done all you can to avoid a shopping binge and still find yourself driving home with packages you can't face, give yourself a break. Is one action or one extended moment of weakness enough to ruin all your plans? Of course it isn't. And brooding over it will simply send you further down the spiral and block recovery. Some ideas:

1. **Forgive yourself.**

2. **Watch your self-talk.** Now is not the time to depress yourself further with self-punishing talk. Don't ever tell yourself you're "out of control." You may put your control on hold for a while, but it is always yours to pick up again. Stick to reality and

celebrate all the positive steps you've taken so far. Feel good, too, about the positive steps you're about to take.

3. Plan your recovery. How will you make up for your lapse? Can this week's budget absorb the expense if you subtract this purchase from another area? Can you count it as next month's splurge? Can you return all or some of the items? Thinking up a concrete idea for fitting this move back into your budget will help you see that it too can be part of forward progress. The trick is to return again to your budget plan.

4. Put it into context. Did you really undo all your progress? That would be unlikely, since your awareness of the problem is still growing and contributing to your self-knowledge and recovery. Remember that real progress is often a matter of "two steps forward, one step back." It may be a frustrating pace, but it moves you forward all the same.

5. See it as a learning opportunity. What happened that led you to break your initial resolve? At what point did you still feel that you could walk away from spending? When did the urge to buy feel inevitable? The more you can learn from this episode, the more control you will gain over yourself and your habit, and the less likely it will happen this way again. Enter your thoughts and revelations into your shopping journal.

Will I Ever Be Free Again?

Yes, it can be tiring to monitor yourself and your habits constantly. And especially tiring to monitor a habit that you once considered a spontaneous joy. But you can believe that it won't always be this way.

The beginning stages of changing old habits are hard. You are asking yourself to let go of trusted supports before the new ones are in place. While you know intellectually that you're making the only sensible move, it may take the rest of your body and soul time to catch up. One woman who had recently broken up with an abusive boyfriend—and felt proud and strong about it—would find her fingers dialing his number on the telephone before she realized it. The urge to hear his familiar, charming voice seemed all-powerful, eclipsing her conscious willpower and desire for change. When she slammed the phone down before he picked it up, grateful that she remembered her resolve to stay away, she still felt a stab of deprivation.

The deprivation comes from the idea that the change is negative, a *taking away*. The ending of the old behavior or relationship leaves a palpable emptiness. But slowly, things rush in to fill the emptiness. Your focus eventually shifts from the absence of the old habit to the presence of the new. This shift can be exhilarating. So many new experiences and relationships come your way because of the change that it feels like a cause for celebration. What's more, by the time this happens, the old habit has generally lost its magical appeal. The wisdom of the change seems obvious, as do most things in retrospect.

It requires a leap of faith at the beginning to believe that you will get to this point at the end. You need to set yourself up to receive the blessings of new habits and act as if you're on your way. The woman who left an abusive relationship acted as if she were not connected to this angry man by not calling him and not seeing him—and she made it so. What's more, she was in a position to meet a new, more appropriate mate. (Which, before long, she did.) By consciously committing yourself to the lifestyle of someone who does not lose valuable time and money shopping, *you will be that person.* What begins as a conscious effort turns gradually into effortless, natural behavior.

Amateur pilots learn that their airplanes must labor with particular difficulty through the first ten feet or so of lift-off. The planes need to escape the "ground effect"—the immediate pull of the earth's magnetic force to keep objects directly on the surface from flying off. Once this forcefield is broken through (and with enough speed and momentum, it is always broken through), the plane flies free. Breaking a habit can feel the same way. Its force can overwhelm you, keeping you stuck tight to its surface. Once you gather the speed and momentum to break away—powered by your simple resolve to change, carried through determinedly for the first few difficult feet—you, too, will be free to soar and land wherever you choose.

Resources

Agencies and organizations that may be able to provide assistance of various kinds.

National Foundation for Consumer Credit
8611 2nd Ave. #100
Silver Spring, MD 20910

National Self-Help Clearinghouse
25 W. 43rd St., Room 620
New York, NY 10036
(212) 642-2944

Debtors Anonymous
P.O. Box 20322
New York, NY 10025
(212) 642-8222

Debtors Anonymous
420 Lexington Ave., #300
New York, NY 10170

National Council for Self-Esteem
P.O. Box 277877
Sacramento, CA 95827
(916) 455-NCSE
(916) 454-2000

Gamblers Anonymous
International Service Office
P.O. Box 17173
Los Angeles, CA 90017
(213) 386-8789

Gam-Anon International Service Office, Inc.
P.O. Box 157
Whitestone, NY 11357
(718) 352-1671

National Council on Problem Gambling, Inc.
445 West 59th St.
New York, NY 10019
(212) 765-3833
Nationwide Help Line: 1-800-522-4700

To curtail your junk mail, contact:
Green Seal
P.O. Box R
Stanford University
Stanford, CA 94309

The following association provides a free service that will remove your name from many direct-mail lists: (Provide every variation of the spelling of your name that has appeared on mailing labels, include names of other family members, allow 3 months for your name to be purged).

Mail Preference Service
c/o Direct Marketing Association
P.O. Box 3861
New York, NY 10163

References

Atlee, Tom. "The Conversion of the American Dream." *Context*, No. 26, 1990, pp. 15-19.

Beattie, Melody. *Codependent No More*. New York: Harper/Hazelden, 1987.

Beck, Aaron. *Cognitive Therapy and the Emotional Disorders*. New York: International Universities Press, Inc., 1976.

Belk, Russell. "Materialism: Trait Aspects of Living in the Material World." *Journal of Consumer Research*, Vol. 12, December 1985, pp. 265-280.

_____. "Possessions and the Extended Self." *Journal of Consumer Research*, Vol. 15, No. 2, September 1988, pp. 139-168.

Berger, John. *Ways of Seeing*. London: BBC, 1972

Bolton, Robert. *People Skills*. New York: Simon and Schuster, Inc., 1979.

Boyd, Harper W. and Levy, Sidney. "New Dimensions in Consumer Analysis." *Harvard Business Review*, Vol. 41, November/December 1963, pp. 129-140.

Bruner, Gordon C. II. "Music, Mood, and Marketing." *Journal of Marketing*, Vol. 54, No. 4, October 1990, pp. 94-104.

Buttle, Francis. "Can You Afford to Ignore Merchandising?" *Management Decision (UK)*, Vol. 25, No. 6, 1987, pp. 14-17.

Carman, John. "First Things First on Trying Day." *The San Francisco Chronicle*, October 22, 1991.

Catalano, Ellen Mohr. *The Chronic Pain Control Workbook*. Oakland, CA: New Harbinger Publications, 1987.

_____. *Getting to Sleep*. Oakland, CA: New Harbinger Publications, 1990.

Cohen, Richard. "Money Matters." *Washington Post Magazine*, September 29, 1991.

Damon, Janet E. *Shopaholics: Serious Help for Addicted Spenders*. Los Angeles: Price Stern Sloan, Inc., 1988.

Davis, Martha; Eschelman, Elizabeth Robbins; and McKay, Matthew. *The Relaxation and Stress Reduction Workbook*. Oakland, CA: New Harbinger Publications, Inc., 1988.

DiGiuseppe, Raymond and McInerney, John. "Patterns of Addiction: A Rational-Emotive Perspective." *Journal of Cognitive Psychotherapy*, Vol. 4, No. 2, 1990, pp. 121-134.

Dominguez, J. *Your Money or Your Life*. New York: Viking/Penguin, 1992.

Douglas, Mary and Isherwood, Baron. *The World of Goods: Towards an Anthropology of Consumption*. New York: W.W. Norton, 1979.

Durgee, Jeffrey F. "Qualitative Methods for Developing Advertising That Makes Consumers Feel, 'Hey, That's Right for Me.'" *Journal of Consumer Marketing*, Vol. 7, Winter 1990, pp. 15-21.

Ehrenreich, Barbara. "The American Family vs. The American Dream: Awash in a Storm of Consumer Choice." *Networker*, September/October 1992, pp. 55-60.

Ewen, Stuart. "Waste A Lot, Want A Lot: Our All-Consuming Quest for Style." *Utne Reader*, September/October 1989, p. 81.

Faber, Ronald J.; O'Guinn, Thomas C.; and Krych, Raymond "Compulsive Consumption." *Advances in Consumer Research*, 1987, pp. 132-135.

Faludi, Susan. *Backlash: The Undeclared War Against American Women*. New York: Crown, 1991.

Fanning, Patrick; McKay, Matthew; and Sonenberg, Nina. *Applied Relaxation Training*. Oakland, CA: New Harbinger Publications, Inc., 1990. Sound Cassette.

"Food Emporium Takes Charge at Checkout." *Chain Store Age Executive*, Vol. 64, No. 12, December 1988, p. 75.

Fox, Richard Wightman, and Lears, T. J. Jackson, eds. *The Culture of Consumption*. New York: Pantheon Books, 1983.

Glaberson, William. "The Heart of the City Now Beats in the Mall." The *New York Times*, March 27, 1992.

Goepel, John. "At the Mall." *Motorland/CSAA Magazine*. March/April 1991, pp. 24-25.

Goldhor Lerner, Harriet. *The Dance of Anger*. New York: Harper and Row, 1985.

Goleman, Daniel. "Reining in a Compulsion to Spend." The *New York Times*, July 17, 1991.

Holbrook, Morris B. and Hirschman, Elizabeth C. "The Experiential Aspects of Consumption: Consumer Fantasies, Feelings, and Fun." *Journal of Consumer Research*, Vol. 9, No. 2, September 1982, pp. 132-140.

Huffman, Vernon. "Getting Past Hawkers. Or, How to Keep Advertisting From Running Your Life." *Context*, No. 26, 1990, pp. 40-41.

Jacoby, Susan. "Compulsive Shopping." *Glamour Magazine*, April, 1986, p. 318.

Jansen, A; Ven den Hout, M.A.; De Loof, C.; Zandbergen, J.; and Griez, E. "A Case of Bulimia Successfully Treated by Cue Exposure." *Journal of Behavior Therapy and Experimental Psychiatry*, Vol. 20 (Great Britian), 1989, pp. 327-332.

Kanner, Bernice. "The Secret Life of the Female Consumer." *Working Woman*, December 1990, pp. 69-71.

Karen, Robert. "Shame." *The Atlantic Monthly*, February 1992, pp. 40-70.

Kaye, Yvonne. *Credit, Cash and Co-Dependency*. Deerfield Beach, FL: Health Communications, Inc., 1991.

"Keeping Your Cool at the Cosmetic Counter." *Glamour*, Vol. 87, September 1989, p. 101.

Kitman, Marvin. *George Washington's Expense Account*. New York: Simon & Schuster, 1970.

_____. *The Making of the President, 1789*. New York: Harper & Row, 1989.

Krueger, David W., M.D. "On Compulsive Shopping and Spending: A Psychodynamic Inquiry." *American Journal of Psychotherapy*, Vol. XLII, October 1988, pp. 574-583.

Lasater, Lane. *Recovery From Compulsive Behavior*. Deerfield Beach, FL: Health Communications, Inc., 1988.

Lawrence, Lauren. "The Psychodynamics of the Female Shopper." *The American Journal of Psychoanalysis*, Vol. 50, March 1990, pp. 67-70.

Levenkron, Steven. *Obsessive-Compulsive Disorders*. New York: Warner Books, 1991.

Macleod. "Phenomenology: A Challenge To Experimental Psychology." *Behaviorism and Phenomenology*, edited by T. W. Wann, Chicago: University of Chicago Press, 1964, pp. 47-78.

Marx, Karl. *Writings of the Young Marx on Philosophy and Society*, Edited by Lloyd D. Easton and Kurt H. Guddat. New York: Doubleday, 1967, 1844, p. 308.

Mellan, Olivia. "Money: The Last Taboo." Networker, March/April 1992, pp. 41-47.

Meyer, Marianne. "Attention, Shoppers!" *Marketing & Media Decisions*, Vol. 23, No. 5, May 1988, pp. 67-70.

Mundis, Jerrold. *How to Get Out of Debt, Stay Out of Debt and Live Prosperously*. New York: Bantam Books, 1988.

Nakken, Craig. *The Addictive Personality: Roots, Rituals, and Recovery.* Minneapolis, MN: Hazelden Foundation, 1988.

Nichols, Michael. *No Place to Hide.* New York: Simon and Schuster, 1991.

O'Guinn, Thomas, and Faber, Ronald. "Compulsive Buying: A Phenomenological Exploration." *Journal of Consumer Research,* Vol. 16, September 1989, pp. 147-157.

O'Neill, Molly. "Taming the Frontier of the Senses: Using Aroma to Manipulate Moods." The *New York Times,* November 27, 1991, p. B1.

Pae, Peter. "Credit Junkies." The *Wall Street Journal,* December. 26, 1991.

Peele, Stanton. *Diseasing of America.* Lexington, MA: D.C. Heath and Co., 1989.

_____. *The Meaning of Addiction: Compulsive Experience and Its Interpretation.* Lexington, MA: D.C. Heath & Co., 1985.

Peterson, Iver. "Americans Confront the Debt the House Built." The *New York Times,* August 11, 1991.

Rice, Berkeley. "The Selling of Life-Styles: Are You What You Buy?" *Psychology Today,* Vol. 22, No. 5, May 1988, pp 46-50.

Robin, Vicki. "Purging the Urge to Splurge." *Context,* No. 26, 1990, pp. 36-39.

Samuelson, Robert J. "The Binge is Over." *Newsweek,* July 10, 1989, p. 35.

Schreiner, Samuel A., Jr. *The Trials of Mrs. Lincoln.* New York: Donald I. Fine, 1987.

Shames, Lawrence. "What a Long, Strange (Shopping) Trip It's Been: Looking Back at the 1980s." *Utne Reader,* September/October 1989, pp. 66-71.

Stein, Benjamin. "The Machine Makes This Man." *Wall Street Journal,* June 13, 1985, p. 30.

Streitfeld, David. "The Addiction Habit: Breaking Step with the Self-Help Movement." The *Washington Post*, August 28, 1990.

Sun, Lena. "Buying Into the Good Life: Spending Cheers Retailers, Worries Financial Planners." The *Washington Post*, November 13, 1988.

Tauber, Edward M. "Why Do People Shop?" Marketing Notes and Communications. *Journal of Marketing*, Vol. 36, No. 4, October 1972, pp. 46-59.

Veblen, Thorstein. *The Theory of the Leisure Class (1899)*. New York: Funk and Wagnalls, 1967.

Wesson, Carolyn. *Women Who Shop Too Much*. New York: St. Martin's Press, 1990.

Whitfield, Charles. *CoDependence: Healing the Human Condition*. Deerfield Beach, FL: Health Communications, 1991.

_____. *Healing the Child Within*. Pompano Beach, FL: Health Communication, 1987.

Other New Harbinger Self-Help Titles

Being a Man: A Guide to the New Masculinity, $12.95
The Deadly Diet, Second Edition: Recovering from Anorexia & Bulimia, $11.95
Last Touch: Preparing for a Parent's Death, $11.95
Consuming Passions: Help for Compulsive Shoppers, $11.95
Self-Esteem, Second Edition, $12.95
Depression & Anxiety Mangement: An audio tape for managing emotional problems, $11.95
I Can't Get Over It, A Handbook for Trauma Survivors, $12.95
Concerned Intervention, When Your Loved One Won't Quit Alcohol or Drugs, $11.95
Redefining Mr. Right, $11.95
Dying of Embarrassment: Help for Social Anxiety and Social Phobia, $11.95
The Depression Workbook: Living With Depression and Manic Depression, $13.95
Risk-Taking for Personal Growth: A Step-by-Step Workbook, $11.95
The Marriage Bed: Renewing Love, Friendship, Trust, and Romance, $11.95
Focal Group Psychotherapy: For Mental Health Professionals, $44.95
Hot Water Therapy: Save Your Back, Neck & Shoulders in 10 Minutes a Day $11.95
Older & Wiser: A Workbook for Coping With Aging, $12.95
Prisoners of Belief: Exposing & Changing Beliefs that Control Your Life, $10.95
Be Sick Well: A Healthy Approach to Chronic Illness, $11.95
Men & Grief: A Guide for Men Surviving the Death of a Loved One., $11.95
When the Bough Breaks: A Helping Guide for Parents of Sexually Abused Childern, $11.95
Love Addiction: A Guide to Emotional Independence, $11.95
When Once Is Not Enough: Help for Obsessive Compulsives, $11.95
The New Three Minute Meditator, $9.95
Getting to Sleep, $10.95
The Relaxation & Stress Reduction Workbook, 3rd Edition, $13.95
Leader's Guide to the Relaxation & Stress Reduction Workbook, $19.95
Beyond Grief: A Guide for Recovering from the Death of a Loved One, $10.95
Thoughts & Feelings: The Art of Cognitive Stress Intervention, $13.95
Messages: The Communication Skills Book, $12.95
The Divorce Book, $11.95
Hypnosis for Change: A Manual of Proven Techniques, 2nd Edition, $12.95
The Chronic Pain Control Workbook, $13.95
Rekindling Desire: Bringing Your Sexual Relationship Back to Life, $12.95
Life Without Fear: Anxiety and Its Cure, $10.95
Visualization for Change, $12.95
Guideposts to Meaning: Discovering What Really Matters, $11.95
Videotape: Clinical Hypnosis for Stress & Anxiety Reduction, $24.95
Starting Out Right: Essential Parenting Skills for Your Child's First Seven Years, $12.95
Big Kids: A Parents' Guide to Weight Control for Children, $11.95
My Parent's Keeper: Adult Children of the Emotionally Disturbed, $11.95
When Anger Hurts, $12.95
Free of the Shadows: Recovering from Sexual Violence, $12.95
Resolving Conflict: With Others and Within Yourself, $12.95
Lifetime Weight Control, $11.95
The Anxiety & Phobia Workbook, $13.95
Love and Renewal: A Couple's Guide to Commitment, $12.95
The Habit Control Workbook, $12.95

Call **toll free, 1-800-748-6273**, to order. Have your Visa or Mastercard number ready. Or send a check for the titles you want to New Harbinger Publications, Inc., 5674 Shattuck Avenue, Oakland, CA 94609. Include $2.00 for the first book and 50¢ for each additional book, to cover shipping and handling. (California residents please include appropriate sales tax.) Allow four to six weeks for delivery.

Prices subject to change without notice.